I HAVE WEATHERED OTHER STORMS

A Response to the Scandals and Democratic Reforms That Threaten the Catholic Church

TFP Committee on American Issues

WESTERN HEMISPHERE CULTURAL SOCIETY
YORK, PENN. 17405

I Have Weathered Other Storms

Amid the storms through which She passes today, the Church could proudly say: "Alios ego vidi ventos; alias prospexi animo procellas" ("*I have already seen other winds and have already weathered other storms*"—Cicero, *Familiares*, 12, 25, 5). *The Church has fought in other lands, against adversaries from among other peoples, and She will undoubtedly continue to face problems and enemies quite different from those of today until the end of time.*

—Plinio Corrêa de Oliveira

Cover photo: Saint Peter's Basilica in Rome. Diego Cinello-Udine, Italy.

The American Society for the Defense of Tradition, Family and Property
1358 Jefferson Road, Spring Grove, Penn. 17362—(717) 225-7147
www.tfp.org

ISBN: 1-881008-04-5
Library of Congress Control Number: 2002116138

Published by
Western Hemisphere Cultural Society, Inc.
P.O. Box 122, York, Penn. 17405

Printed in the United States of America

—Contents—

Office of the Bishop
DIOCESE OF BAKER
Box 5999
Bend, Oregon 97708

October 28, 2002

Mr. Thomas J. McKenna
Tradition, Family and Property
1358 Jefferson Road
Spring Grove, PA 17362

Dear Thomas,

Thank you for entrusting me with one of your latest works, *I Have Weathered Other Storms*. As you can imagine I am very pleased with the clarity and directness of your approach. In the span of a relatively limited number of pages you manage to cover a vast amount of territory and put into a proper Catholic perspective many of the discussions taking place within and outside of the Church. I did find the reading of this text both refreshing and invigorating. Each chapter gives a very clear and accurate enunciation of the Church's teaching. It is this teaching with which I have grown up and which I have held from my youth. It is this teaching which I hope to continue to announce ever more clearly and directly in the months and years to come.

Thank you for being a voice of the Faithful which is an authentically Faithful Lay Catholic voice and not a voice claiming some new counter-magisterial personal revelation.

Asking every good grace and blessing of God upon you, I am

Sincerely Yours in Christ Jesus,

+ Robert F. Vasa

The Most Reverend Robert F. Vasa
Bishop of Baker

Preface

Over the years, many voices have denounced the homosexual movement's inroads into the Catholic Church and its nefarious consequences for both the Mystical Body of Christ and America.[1]

In 1997, the American Society for the Defense of Tradition, Family and Property (TFP) added its own voice to this largely ignored chorus when it reported on Bishop Matthew Clark's Mass for homosexuals and lesbians in Sacred Heart Cathedral in Rochester (March 1, 1997) and on the New Ways Ministry's 4th National Symposium in Pittsburgh (March 7-9, 1997). The American TFP published "Is Sodomy No Longer a Sin? An Urgent Appeal to Our Ecclesiastical Authorities" in *The Wanderer* on April 24, 1997.[2]

In January 2002, the media began a massive campaign of sustained reporting on the sexual scandals by priests and the way bishops handled these crimes over the years. The media's barrage was successful in riveting the nation's attention. Press Secretary Ari Fleischer was asked during a press briefing if President Bush believed grand juries, State Attorney Generals, and district attorneys were wrong in considering prosecution of Church officials for aiding and abetting clergy pedophilia.[3] Indeed, when President Bush visited John Paul II at the Vatican, in May, he expressed the nation's malaise: "I will tell

1. See, for example, Fr. Enrique T. Rueda, *The Homosexual Network: Private Lives and Public Policy* (Old Greenwich, Conn.: The Devin Adair Company, 1982).
2. See Appendix A. In May 1997, TFP Vice-President Thomas J. McKenna took copies of this paper and a detailed report with abundant photographs to the Vatican and delivered them to the Congregation for the Doctrine of the Faith, the Secretariat of State to His Holiness, the Congregation for Bishops, the Pontifical Academy for Life, and the Pontifical Council for the Family. In June 1999, the Vatican Congregation for the Doctrine of the Faith silenced Fr. Robert Nugent and Sr. Jeanine Gramick, the founders of New Ways Ministry, but this had little impact on the homosexual movement's continued subversion of the Church.
3. Cf. April 16, 2002, Press briefing by Ari Fleischer, www.whitehouse.gov/news/releases/2002/04/print/20020416-5.html

[the Pope] that I am concerned about the Catholic Church in America, I'm concerned about its standing. I say that because the Catholic Church is an incredibly important institution in our country."[4] The media made the crisis a concern for America in general.

Being a civic organization of Catholic inspiration,[5] the attention of the American TFP is customarily turned to the consideration of temporal affairs and has not taken an official position on many problems of a strictly theological nature. The present crisis, however, while religious in origin, has had uncontestable impact on the temporal sphere. Bill O'Reilly summarized it well:

> The damage to the world in this case is incalculable. We live in a time of moral relativism, where many human beings simply will not make judgments about right and wrong. President Clinton was a poster-boy for this group. All behavior can be explained, and most excused. Evil is a word, not a force.... Many people, perhaps most, do not believe what the Church proclaims. But the fact that there was a force in the world that would present an argument for absolute behavior was very important. The relativists of the world often will not demand responsibility for personal behavior that injures other people. The Church does demand that. And the world

4. Ron Fournier, "Bush, Pope Discuss Sex Scandals," *The Detroit News*, May 29, 2002.
5. "[The TFP] is a civic, cultural and nonpartisan organization which, inspired by the traditional teachings of the Supreme Magisterium of the Roman Catholic Church, works in a legal and peaceful manner in the realm of ideas to defend and promote the principles of private ownership, family and perennial Christian values with their twofold function: individual and social." The Foundation for a Christian Civilization, Inc., Bylaws, Art. 1, § 2.

> needs to hear that point of view, or it will be engulfed in a secularism that can severely weaken even the strongest societies. Hello, ancient Rome."[6]

In such circumstances, the American TFP felt obliged in conscience[7] to add its voice to the many being heard in the public square and address the unfolding crisis. On April 11, the American TFP published in *The Washington Times* a position paper "In Face of the Scandals, the Church, Holy and Immortal, Shall Prevail."[8] This paper does not deny that scandalous behavior occurred, but focuses on its deeper causes and lists reasons for hope that can serve to strengthen the Faith. This was published in The Washington Times on April 11 and later in ten other newspapers. A leaflet edition in both English and Spanish was also printed for parish distribution. As this book goes to press, 1.2 million copies are in circulation and the TFP has received words of appreciation and support for this effort from two cardinals, 25 bishops, 246 priests, and 200 nuns.

At the June meeting of the American bishops in Dallas, the TFP published "Pressure Groups Push for Revolution Inside the Church" in the June 13 edition of *The Dallas Morning*

6. Bill O'Reilly, "An Easter Message for the Catholic Church," www.townhall.com/columnists/billoreilly/printbo20020330.shtml.
7. Canon 212, § 3—"In accord with the knowledge, competence and preeminence which they [the Christian faithful] possess, they have the right and even at times a duty to manifest to the sacred pastors their opinion on matters which pertain to the good of the Church, and they have a right to make their opinion known to the other Christian faithful, with due regard for the integrity of faith and morals and reverence towards their pastors, and with consideration for the common good and dignity of persons." *The Code of Canon Law: A Text and Commentary* James A. Coriden, Thomas J. Green, and Donald E. Heintschel, eds. (New York: Paulist Press, 1985), p. 146.

   Cf. John Paul II, Apostolic Exhortation Christi fideles laici, Dec. 30, 1988; The Benedictine Monks of Solesmes, *The Lay Apostolate, Papal Teachings* (Boston: St. Paul Editions, 1961).
8. See Appendix B.

News.[9] This ad reproduced the TFP's June 1 letter to the bishops alerting them to efforts by Voice of the Faithful (VOTF) and other pressure groups to capitalize on the sexual-abuse crisis to promote their reformist agenda.

The TFP's concerns were well founded. On July 20, Voice of the Faithful held its first national convention in Boston with 4,200 people in attendance. Six speakers were professors at Jesuit universities and other centers of higher learning. Two speakers were married "ex-priests." Several others came from such reformist movements as the Association for the Rights of Catholics in the Church, Call to Action, CORPUS, and We Are Church. These groups advocate a desacralized, egalitarian, and democratic Church, the ordination of women, and an end to priestly celibacy.

At the talks and workshops, VOTF speakers promoted the total democratization of the Church, using the American system of government as a model. They proclaimed the demise of the hierarchical Church and demanded ecclesiastical power for the laity. Fr. Thomas Doyle, O.P., who received VOTF's first "Priest of Integrity Award," delivered the keynote speech. His address was a kind of "Declaration of Independence" in which he outlined the principles buttressing the reformist agenda and stated unequivocally that the "medieval model" of a "monarchical Church" was in its death throes. The presence and testimony of several sexual-abuse victims added great emotional charge to the convention. Their personal tragedy was transformed into a battering ram aimed at toppling the Church's hierarchical structure.

In this book, the American TFP seeks to dispel the confusion and climate of intense emotion that warps the debate and hinders a true solution to the crisis. This is done by succinctly

9. See Appendix C.

stating the Catholic principles and doctrines challenged in the current fracas. These include:

- why Our Lord permits crises in the Church
- why the presence of sinners among the faithful, even among the clergy, does not taint the holiness of the Church
- why the Church is monarchical and hierarchical and not democratic
- the origins and reasons for clerical celibacy
- the office of bishop
- a theological-historical analysis showing the impossibility of women priests
- the use of the sexual-abuse victims in psychological warfare by reformists
- the media's role in the present crisis

In addressing these issues, the American TFP is exercising a right recognized by the Code of Canon Law[10] and an imperative duty of conscience as faithful sons of the Church.

Christ founded His Church upon Peter and the Apostles. However, as Saint Paul made clear to the Corinthians,[11] the Church does not belong to anyone other than to Christ Himself.

May the Blessed Virgin Mary bless this effort, which seeks nothing but Her glory and, thus, that of Her Divine Son, and the liberty and exaltation of Holy Mother Church.

10. Cf. Canon 212, § 3.
11. 1 Cor. 3:5-7.

INTRODUCTION

Our Lord Always Watches Over His Church, but Allows Her to Be Rocked by Crises

The Church is often pictured as Peter's Bark sailing on the seas of history.

Sometimes calm winds fill Her sails and She skims over the waves with lofty and serene grace. At other times, however, the winds howl, the sea churns with frothy waves, lightning bolts crisscross the skies, thunder alarms the sailors, and the ship appears to be sinking.

As the roaring squall tosses Peter's Bark about, the Savior sleeps. With the Apostles, we cry out: "Lord, save us for we perish!" Awakening, Jesus reassures us as He did them: "Why are you fearful, O ye of little faith?" He stands up and in an imposing voice orders the storm to cease and quiets the sea.[1]

"IT IS IMPOSSIBLE THAT SCANDALS SHOULD NOT COME"

Today the Church is buffeted by sexual-abuse scandals and cover-ups by ecclesiastical authorities. She is under attack by Her enemies, while uncertainty and confusion shake Her children.

Many do not understand why Our Lord seems to sleep or why He allows evil to penetrate the sanctuary. It apparently contradicts both the Church's promised indefectibility and the holiness of the Mystical Spouse of Christ. Their faith wavers: If the Church is not holy, She cannot be the true Church of Christ.

Others react by seeking to reform the Church, blaming the crisis on Her tenets, teachings, and Divinely instituted hierarchical structure.

1. Matt. 8:25-26.

Sometimes Our Lord seems to sleep amid the storms that assail Peter's Bark. But He sleeps not, and if He permits the tempests to roar, it is to purify our Faith of all human attachment.

Our Lord promises that the gates of Hell would not prevail against the Church,[2] and that He will assist Her daily to the end of time.[3] However, He does not promise that She would not undergo crises, scandals, and apparent failures.

Much to the contrary, Our Lord's parables about the Kingdom of God, which is His Church, clearly affirmed that good and bad alike would be part of Her until the end of time. Only then will God send His angels to cleanse the earth of scandal.[4]

This earthly life is a period of trial. Thus, some will do evil and give scandal to others. "It is impossible that scandals should not come," says Our Lord, "but woe to him through whom they come!"[5] Saint Paul explains how these scandals help purify our Faith: "For there must be also heresies: that they also, who are approved, may be made manifest among you."[6]

God permits temptation, but He always provides sufficient grace to resist. Saint Paul teaches: "God is faithful, who will not suffer you to be tempted above that which you are able: but will make also with temptation issue, that you may be able to bear it."[7]

Expounding on the episode of Our Lord asleep in the boat, Saint John Chrysostom explains that the storm symbolizes the Church's future trials, during which the faithful, the athletes of Christ, will be fortified. After quoting Saint John Chrysostom, Cornelius a Lapide, the distinguished Scripture commentator, cites Seneca to show that even a pagan writer understood the spiritual gain accrued from the struggle against temptation: "Life without temptation is like a dead sea."[8]

2. Matt. 16:17-19.
3. Matt. 28:18-20.
4. Matt. 13 (*in toto*).
5. Luke 17:1.
6. 1 Cor. 11:19.
7. 1 Cor. 10:13.
8. Cornelius a Lapide, *Commentaria in Scripturam Sacram* (Paris: Vivès, 1881), Vol. 15, p. 234.

The Church is the "House of God" whose cornerstone is Christ.[9] It is "the Holy City, the New Jerusalem" brought down from Heaven.[10] However, God permits temptations even inside this sacred place, as our first parents were tested in the Earthly Paradise. In this way, our love is purged of all attachments to divine consolation and human concerns.

THE LORD HIMSELF FORETOLD SCANDALS

Saint Augustine explains that there will always be some bishops resembling the Good Shepherd and others representing the Hireling. He wrote to Felicia, a virgin who grieved over the scandals then plaguing the Church:

> I exhort you not to let yourself be too much troubled by scandals, which indeed were foretold precisely so that when they happen we may remember that they were foretold and not be disconcerted. For the Lord Himself foretold them in the Gospel. "Woe to the world because of scandals. For it must needs be that scandals come: but nevertheless, woe to that man by whom the scandal cometh" (Matt. 18:7).... Thus, there are those who hold the office of shepherds that they may watch over Christ's sheep; and there are those who hold it for the sake of temporal honors and worldly advantages. These two kinds of pastors, always dying and giving place to others, will both be perpetuated in the bosom of the Catholic Church till time ends and the Lord comes to judgment.[11]

9. 1 Cor. 3:9, 11; Matt. 21:42.
10. Apoc. 21:2.
11. Epist. 208, 2 and 5, in Charles Cardinal Journet, *The Church of the Word Incarnate* (New York: Sheed and Ward, 1955), pp. 97-98.

Finally, facing the errors of Luther and Calvin, the Church affirmed that She is not a "Church of Saints" or "Church of the Predestined" but holds within Her bosom both just men and sinners.[12]

The history of the Church shows clearly that She has always undergone trials. At the very beginning, fierce persecutions sought to destroy Her from without. Immediately afterwards, heresy assailed Her from within.

At the dawn of the fourth century, the Church had to contend with Arianism, one of the most devastating heresies. Arianism denied the divinity of Our Lord and claimed that Jesus was a mere (albeit more perfect) creature, created by the Father to be the divine intermediary in the creation and redemption of the world. However, Arius, the heresy's founder, affirmed that His nature was not of the same substance as the Father, that the Son was not *consubstantial* with the Father.

This heresy attacked the very foundations of Christianity. If the Word were not divine, God did not become man, and the mysteries of the Incarnation, Passion, Death, and Resurrection of Our Lord would have no transcendental meaning.

This heresy spread throughout the entire Christian world. So many bishops adhered to it that Saint Jerome exclaimed with rhetorical hyperbole: "The whole world groaned and marveled to find itself Arian."[13]

SPIRITUAL HOMICIDE AND SUICIDE

In a sermon on the present scandals, Fr. Roger J. Landry, pastor of Espirito Santo parish in Fall River, Mass., opportunely observes: "Scandal is unfortunately nothing new for the

12. Fr. Joachim Salaverri, S.J., *De Ecclesia Christi*, in VV.AA, *Sacrae Theologiae Summa*, (Madrid: Biblioteca de Autores Cristianos, 1958), Vol. I, no. 1128, p. 912.
13. William Barry, *s.v.* "Arianism," *Catholic Encyclopedia* (1913), Vol. I, p. 710.

Church.... At each of the times when the Church hit its low point, God raised up tremendous saints to bring the Church back to its real mission. It's almost as if in those times of darkness, the Light of Christ shone ever more brightly."

Father Landry mentions the bad example of Pope Alexander VI during the Renaissance. He fathered several children from various concubines and later enriched his children with Church property. Many were scandalized and shaken in their Faith. Luther revolted, apostatized, and started a new religion. Father Landry notes: "Eventually God raised up many saints to combat this wrong solution and to bring people back to the Church Christ founded. Saint Francis de Sales was one of them."

After mentioning heroic episodes in the life of Saint Francis, Father Landry quotes the saint: "While those who commit these types of scandals are guilty of the spiritual equivalent of murder, those who take scandal—who allow scandals to destroy their faith—are guilty of spiritual suicide."

Concluding, Father Landry says that Saint Francis "went among the people in what is now Switzerland trying to prevent their committing spiritual suicide on account of the scandals. I'm here to preach the same thing to you."[14]

14. Fr. Roger J. Landry, *Answering Scandal with Personal Holiness*, in Catholic Educator's Resource Center www.catholiceducation.org/articles/religion/re0526.html, 2002.

CHAPTER 1

Examining the Role of the Media

On January 6, 2002, *The Boston Globe* fired its first broadside in what would become a massive campaign denouncing the sexual scandals inside the Church. By March, most of the national media were seconding these efforts. Any attempt to count the tens of thousands of written articles, television and radio newscasts, and talk show sessions on the scandals would be a grueling task.

ARE THE MEDIA SAVING THE CHURCH?

The Catholic reaction to this media blitz varies.

Some Catholics are unconcerned and attribute it to the journalist's pursuit of a good story to boost newspaper circulation.

However, far too many Catholics, including numerous conservatives, believe the media are rendering a great service to the Church. Without media pressure, they say, the bishops will not bother to take effective measures and the scandals will continue and spread. Unfortunately, the large number of real scandals and the role played by ecclesiastical authorities are mainly responsible for this attitude.

Liberal Catholics rejoice at the media's sustained coverage and seize the opportunity to push for reform. Old groups and newly established ones see the crisis as a way to promote their agenda. Among the new groups is Voice of the Faithful (VOTF).[1] Friendly media soon trumpeted VOTF's ambiguous and contradictory slogan, "Keep the Faith, Change the Church," around the country.

At VOTF's first convention in Boston on July 20, 2002, the

1. See Chapter 3.

keynote speaker, Fr. Thomas Doyle, lavishly praised the media's role in the Church crisis.

Another speaker, James Carroll, a married priest and *Boston Globe* journalist, called the media coverage "a grace," repeating what he had written earlier in his regular column in the *Globe*: "Beginning with *The Boston Globe*'s revelations in January...newspaper coverage of this crisis has been what must be called a grace."[2]

Some observers wonder why liberal journalists, many of whom tolerate or even advocate homosexuality,[3] are so eager to denounce the sexual scandals inside the Church. They suspect the homosexual movement[4] has something to gain by exposing these scandals.

REPORTERS ALSO HAVE ORIGINAL SIN

In following the media's coverage, the media cannot be considered larger-than-life, superhuman entities free from the defects and limitations of all things human. Like society, the media are made up of individuals with their own desires, pho-

2. James Carroll, "A Letter to the Bishops," *The Boston Globe*, June 11, 2002.
3. In opposition to a usage that is becoming generalized, we restrict the term "homosexuality" to homosexual practices, thus excluding the mere inclination. No individual who suffers from such unnatural inclination and resists it with the help of grace can be called a "homosexual," just as no one who resists the inclination to steal or lie can be called a "thief" or a "liar."
4. We deliberately avoid using the word "gay"unless in quoting others. Our reason for this is that we believe that the accepted and universal use of the word "gay" would constitute a victory for the homosexual ideology. Moreover, the word "gay" connotes joy, but a vice that Catholic doctrine refers to as an aberration against nature cannot possibly give true joy or happiness.

   Livio Melina, Moral Theology professor at the Pontifical Lateran University in Rome, makes an important observation on "gay culture": "Today this term [the homosexual expression "gay"] is highly politicized and does not simply mean a homosexually oriented person but one who publicly adopts a homosexual 'lifestyle' and is committed to having it accepted by society as fully legitimate. Justifiable opposition to offences and discrimination, which violate a person's basic rights, cannot be confused with this demand. In fact a systematic

bias, special interests, religious beliefs, and ideologies.

To assume that journalists, by the simple fact that they are journalists, report from inside a vacuum untainted by any influence would be to consider them somehow above human nature or perhaps conceived without Original Sin. Such assumptions appear analogous to Rousseau's unrealistic concept of the "noble savage."

Indeed, the media also are capable of bias, a fact that has been repeatedly documented.[6] The question naturally arises whether the media's coverage of the present scandals is fair, or if it somehow advances specific agendas.

THE HOMOSEXUAL MOVEMENT ALSO INFLUENCES THE MEDIA

One of these agendas found in many media is that of the homosexual movement.

Just as the movement's influence on society grew enormously after the 1969 Stonewall Riot, the media were not immune to this same influence.

A quick perusal of the website of the National Lesbian & Gay Journalists Association (NLGJA) demonstrates just how active the homosexual movement is in the media. There one reads:

> Since its founding in 1990, NLGJA has grown to a

plan for the public justification and glorification of homosexuality is taking shape, starting with the attempt to make it fully accepted in the mind of society. It aims, through increasing pressure, at a change in legislation so that homosexual unions may enjoy the same rights as marriage, including that of adoption." Livio Melina, "Christian Anthropology and Homosexuality—Moral Criteria for Evaluating Homosexuality," *L'Osservatore Romano* (weekly edition in English), Mar. 12, 1997, p. 5.

5. See, for example, Bernard Goldberg, *Bias: A CBS Insider Exposes How the Media Distorts the News* (Washington, D.C.: Regnery Publishing, Inc., 2002). A

> 1,100-member, 22-chapter organization in the United States with affiliations in Canada and Germany. The issues of same-sex marriage, gay families, parenting and adoption, gays in the military, sex education in the schools, civil liberties, gay-related ballot initiatives, gay bashing and anti-gay violence are commanding media attention with regularity. NLGJA has had a positive effect on responsible gay coverage, but we still have work to do.[5]

THE MEDIA HELP SHAPE OPINIONS

This unrelenting "responsible gay coverage" in the media is largely accountable for society's growing acceptance of the homosexual agenda. Children's television producer Nickelodeon, for example, recently aired "My Family Is Different" to the elation of the Gay & Lesbian Alliance Against Defamation (GLAAD). In its press release, GLAAD states:

> "Thank Nickelodeon For Airing Smart Kids'-Eye View of LGBT Families"—Children's cable network Nickelodeon aired a groundbreaking and long-overdue news program last night entitled, "Nick News Special Edition: My Family Is Different." Produced by Linda Ellerbee's Lucky Duck Productions and hosted by Ellerbee, "My Family Is Different" featured children of

recent survey by the Pew Research Center revealed a fall of public confidence in the media when compared to the levels reached during the coverage of the September 11 events: 56 percent of those surveyed said the media usually report inaccurately, and only 35 percent thought the media usually get the facts straight; two-thirds said that the media try to cover up their mistakes; 59 percent believe the media are politically biased and only 26 percent say they were careful to avoid bias (Reed Irvine, "Stinking Coverage of Pew Poll," *CommentMax—NewsMax.com*, Aug. 12, 2002).

6. Cf. www.nlgja.org/about/about.html.

> gay and lesbian parents talking with children from households that oppose equal rights for gay and lesbian families about the issues that affect their lives, including hate speech, bullying and harassment. Among the other participants on the show: openly lesbian parent Rosie O'Donnell; Tom Ryan, a New York City firefighter who is also a gay father; and Mark French, an openly gay school principal.[7]

GLAAD was equally jubilant after convincing *The New York Times* to start announcing homosexual partnerships and civil unions side by side with traditional marriages in its "Weddings and Celebrations" section.[8]

MOCKING THE CHURCH: "CAN THE CHURCH BE SAVED?"

A second undercurrent in media is an anti-Catholic bias.

The cover of the April 1, 2002, issue of *Time* magazine shows the back of a clergyman, probably a bishop, enveloped in shadows. The headline reads, "Can the Catholic Church Save Itself?" The inside heading goes further, asking, "Can the Church Be Saved?"[9]

Time's approach does not seek to help the Catholic faithful persevere in this massive crisis. Rather, it fosters despondency and doubts about the Faith.

Time's mockery continues in a section titled "Catholicism in Crisis," where there appears the article "The Confession of

7. www.glaad.org/org/news/alerttoday/index.html?record=3032.
8. www.glaad.org/org/prss/index.html?record+3044, Aug. 28, 2002.
9. *Time* has long advocated the homosexual agenda. The cover story of its April 14, 1997, issue featured actress Ellen Degeneres, who had just "outed," presenting her as "Breaking Another TV Taboo." *Time*'s use of this word suggests that people's natural revulsion for homosexuality is not a moral imperative but a mere inhibition resulting from social custom or emotional aversion.

Father X," in which an anonymous former priest describes in detail how he abused children.

The same issue has another article titled "What the Nuns Didn't Know" by Margaret Carlson. She repeats the thesis of many so-called Catholic feminists and cites Sr. Joan Chittister, one of the current's leaders.[10] She also advocates the ordination of women as a solution to the present crisis:

> What a shame. If nuns had had higher status, they might have prevented the cover-up.... The all-male power structure of the church employed the worst tactics of its secular counterparts: silencing victims, covering up crimes, shifting bad priests around like fungible account executives.... Perhaps this will inspire Pope John Paul, or his successor, to see the wisdom of admitting women to the priesthood.[11]

"SINNER VS. SINNER: WHOSE IS BIGGER?"

Another example of the liberal media's derision of the Catholic Church is Joan Vennochi's *Boston Globe* article titled "Sinner vs. Sinner: Whose Is Bigger?" Ms. Vennochi saunters into the realm of moral theology with little knowledge of Catholic doctrine. Her thesis is that since bishops are also sinners, they cannot reprimand the laity, for sin puts them on equal footing. An editorial in Boston's archdiocesan paper accused Oklahoma Gov. Frank Keating of urging Catholics "to commit a mortal sin" by skipping Sunday Mass as a protest against lax diocesan sexual-abuse policies. Ms. Vennochi wrote:

10. Cf. www.eriebenedictines.org/benetvision/discipleshiptalk.html; Also see, Donna Steichen, *Ungodly Rage: The Hidden Face of Catholic Feminism* (San Francisco: Ignatius Press, 1991).
11. *Time*, April 1, 2002.

The liberal media's harsh questioning of the Church's indefectibility contrasts with their glowing sympathy for homosexual behavior.

> But the thinking Catholic cannot help but wonder, what is the bigger sin? Failing to attend Mass or failing to protect children?
>
> This is what the church hierarchy, still exemplified most diligently by Cardinal Bernard Law, still doesn't understand. Catholics are ranking their sins against those of their leaders and deciding that when it comes to sin, they are at least equals. This sin-to-sinner assessment may even lead some—not all—Catholic lay people to conclude they are more virtuous than their priests. So why should they listen to them?[12]

Perhaps unwittingly, Ms. Vennochi falls into a kind of neo-Donatism whereby sinful clergymen lose their authority over the faithful.[13]

A MOVEMENT'S PRESSURE TO PACKAGE THE NEWS...

These two biases find common ground in the current scandals.

One cannot help but notice the great pains taken by much of the media in their reporting of the sexual scandals to exempt homosexuality from all blame. This does not happen by chance. It illustrates the media's responsiveness to the homosexual lobby and the activism of many homosexuals within the media.

12. Joan Vennochi, "Sinner vs. Sinner: Whose Is Bigger?" *The Boston Globe*, Aug. 13, 2002.
13. The Donatist heresy denied the validity of sacraments administered by sinful priests. Saint Augustine refuted this heresy by demonstrating how the efficacy of the sacraments derives from the sanctity of Our Lord Jesus Christ and not the virtue of His ministers. (Cf. "Donatism" in Cardinals Pietro Parente, Antonio Piolanti, Salvatore Garofalo, *Dictionary of Dogmatic Theology* [Milwaukee: Bruce Publishing Company, 1952], p. 82.) Similarly, ecclesiastical authority does not come from the sanctity of bishops, but from the power given them by Christ to govern the flock. This authority is not lost by sin, but solely through the loss

A case in point is the commentary of GLAAD activist Cathy Renna about the bishops' June 2002 meeting in Dallas. She refers to her lobbying of the media to counter the efforts of Bishop Fabian Bruskewitz and conservative organizations to highlight the homosexual element in the scandals. She writes:

> The conversations I had with reporters in Dallas this week showed me that we've clearly turned a corner in terms of the waning credibility of those attacks. The media I spoke with this week are seeing right through them. They're seeking out experts on child sexual abuse who are making abundantly clear the distinctions between healthy gay and straight sexuality and any tendency toward sexual abuse. They're talking to gay and straight victims of the abuse. And they're recognizing that LGBT Catholics and gay priests—and their stories—have important roles to play in the ongoing process of healing, reform and accountability.[14]

... AND PROTECT HOMOSEXUALITY IN THE SEMINARIES

Activist Renna further explains that the homosexual movement will do everything it can to frustrate attempts to eradicate

of ecclesiastical office, in accordance with appropriate Church Law (voluntary resignation; a resignation submitted to and accepted by Church authority because of old age; expiration of the period for which he was appointed; transfer to another jurisdiction; removal from office by Church authority; removal from office by the law itself for reasons of heresy and schism. Cf. Canons 184, 194 § 1, n. 2; 1364 § 1; 1336 § 1 nn. 1-3.). Thus it would be an error analogous to the Donatist heresy to sustain that one should only obey holy shepherds and that bishops who sin automatically lose their authority.

14. GLAAD Media Briefing From The U.S. Bishops' Conference In Dallas—June 15, 2002 *News Update: Day Three: Wrapping Up*, http://www.glaad.org/org/publications/documents/index.html?record=3023.

homosexuality from American seminaries:

> With the Apostolic Visitations of U.S. seminaries expected to begin in August (and expected to last for two years), *Dignity/USA and other church reform groups* are going to be monitoring to see whether Vatican leaders will quietly attempt to purge gay men from the priesthood. GLAAD will be working closely with Dignity and our respective contacts inside the church to make sure the media are closely monitoring the process and outcomes of these visitations.[15]

MEDIA BLITZ ADVANCES THE HOMOSEXUAL AGENDA...

She further states that the media coverage of the scandals has been helpful to the homosexual cause. At a Dignity Mass celebrated in the "Cathedral of Hope,"[16] she reports meeting with Anne Barrett Doyle, a VOTF leader and a representative of the Coalition of Concerned Catholics,[17] another pressure group founded because of the crisis:

> I had the pleasure of finally meeting Anne Barrett Doyle of the Coalition of Concerned Catholics (and a member of the steering committee for the lay reform movement Voice of the Faithful). Anne was one of the first people I spoke with back in March

15. Ibid. Our emphasis.
16. The "Cathedral of Hope" claims to be "the world's largest liberal Christian church with predominantly gay, lesbian, and transgendered outreach." Founded in 1970, it claims to have 3,000 members. (www.cathedralofhope.com/press/phase3.htm).
17. This group's new name is the Coalition of Catholics and Survivors. Cf. Michael S. Rosenwald, "At Mass, Cardinal Mum on Sex Abuse," *The Boston Globe*, June 3, 2002.

> when we were cultivating resources and contacts to offer media outlets.
>
> Seeing Anne at the cathedral brought to mind *how far we've come in the past months*. Although anti-gay activists and far-right commentators (and church officials like Bishop Bruskewitz) continue to seize on this crisis, the public increasingly have gotten wise to their antics.[18]

...IN SOCIETY AND IN THE CHURCH

As noted above, *The Boston Globe* has played a leading role in the media campaign against the Church. In March, it published an article by Chuck Colbert, an apparently homosexual seminarian at the Weston Jesuit School of Theology and a Dignity member, whose articles are published in both the liberal Catholic and homosexual press.[19] Mr. Colbert's opinion is that the present scandals favor the homosexual agenda inside the Church. He says:

> The scandal of clerical sexual abuse in the Roman Catholic Church has had a widespread ripple effect in recent weeks, prompting increasingly frank and free-

18. Ibid. Our emphasis.
19. According to *Dignity/USA Dateline* November 1999, Vol. 8, no. 11, Mr. Colbert is a Boston member of the homosexual group Dignity. Also, one reads in *Windy City Times*, Apr. 3, 2002: "'Having covered the crisis in the local church in Boston for the *National Catholic Reporter* and as a layman and seminarian at the Weston Jesuit School of Theology, I am deeply concerned about some of the misleading charges by those attempting to link the abuse of children and young adults with gay men in the priesthood,' said Chuck Colbert. 'The truth is that the sexual abuse of children is criminal, pathological, and sinful. Being gay and living outside of the closet is none of those, as so many of us faithful gay and lesbian Catholics, our families and friends bear witness to every day in our church and in communities across this country." (www.outlineschicago.com/0outlines/apr3~02/nnews.html).

wheeling discussions about human sexuality and gender. The topic of gay priests, gay men, and lesbians in the life of the church is suddenly front and center.

While the idea of ordaining women raises hierarchical blood pressure, the increasing presence of gay Catholics—and significant number of gay priests—triggers near apoplexy in some church officials.

Gay priests and laity are vital to the church's apostolic mission.... Increasingly, pressures from within and without are challenging church doctrine and pastoral practices on sexuality and ministering to gay Catholics.[20]

A COMMON DENOMINATOR OF LIBERAL MEDIA AND CHURCH REFORMIST GROUPS

Chuck Colbert's article also comments on a Louisville seminar by New Ways Ministry called "Out of Silence God Has Called Us: Lesbian/Gay Issues and the Vatican II Church." Mr. Colbert writes:

> Before the symposium got underway, Vatican officials directed local Archbishop Thomas Kelly to forbid the saying of Mass at the event. After consulting with canon lawyers, however, New Ways leaders determined that they did not need permission to celebrate Mass. Wearing a rainbow-colored alb as he officiated, retired Bishop Leroy Matthiesen of Texas was the image of solidarity with gay Catholics. Rainbow-colored banners—visible symbols of the gay commu-

20. Chuck Colbert, "The Spectrum of Belief—The Dialogue on Gays in the Catholic Priesthood Is Also Casting New Light on the Needs of a Far Larger Group: Gays in the Congregation," *The Boston Globe*, Mar. 31, 2002.

> nity and pride—graced the background setting for the liturgy.
>
> The Rev. Ralph Parthie, a Franciscan, spoke of "the turmoil inside of me for a long time" before coming to full self-acceptance of a gay identity.
>
> A closing session featured Gregory Baum, a religious studies professor emeritus at McGill University. Baum, a key figure at the liberalizing Second Vatican Council, focused on homosexual love and the church's natural law tradition. "The entire teaching of sexuality must be reviewed," Baum said, "before the church undertakes any serious consideration of gay love or marriage for gays…"
>
> [Bishop Thomas] Gumbleton said, "We don't put people out of the church for following their conscience."[21]

The cover story of the June 17, 2002, issue of *Time* reports on "Catholics in Revolt." This issue also carries other articles favoring Voice of the Faithful and similar reformist groups as well as a long article analyzing the crisis in the Church and backing the homosexual agenda. An article by Andrew Sullivan, who calls himself a Catholic homosexual, claims the solution for the Church is to "listen to lay people" in moral matters. In his article titled "Who Says the Church Can't Change? An Anguished Catholic Argues That Loving the Church Means Reforming It," Mr. Sullivan writes:

> We kneel and pray; we donate our time and money; we have attempted to explain the moral lessons we have learned in the real world of family and sex and work and conflict. But so many church lead-

21. Ibid.

> ers—from the Pope on down—do not seem to hear or even care. And why should they? They are not answerable to us.[22]

Therefore, Pope and bishops must be made "answerable" to the laity. In an inversion of roles directly opposed to what Our Lord Jesus Christ instituted, the laity replaces the clergy as the true authority in the Church. This echoes the line of Voice of the Faithful and other reformist groups. Mr. Sullivan further claims in his article that Church moral teaching dealing with divorcees, homosexuals, women, and priestly celibacy is absurd and out of touch with the "real world."

Another homosexual organization, GLAAD, supports the same changes of a disciplinary and doctrinal nature in the Church proposed by the reformist groups.

Under the section "Resources for Covering the Catholic Church Sex-Abuse Crisis," GLAAD's website carries an article titled "Nailing Our Demands to the Door of the Catholic Church" by Marcos McPeek Villatory.[23]

The article has the air of a manifesto. Mr. Villatory asks, "What do we want?" and answers:

> "Anything that will bust down the doors of the good-old-boy Roman Catholic hierarchy. Married priests. Women priests. Women bishops. And of course, the abolition of mandated celibacy. We want a new theology of sexuality, one that does not shame Catholics with puritanical teachings that inevitably lead to a stunted sexual development among our pastors."

These revealing words demonstrate how wary one must be

22. Andrew Sullivan, *Time*, June 17, 2002, pp. 63-64.
23. www.glaad.org/org/relations/reference/index.html?record=3009. This article was originally published in *The Los Angeles Times* on June 10, 2002.

of the media's approach to the present scandals.

WHY IS THE MEDIA ATTACKING THE CATHOLIC CHURCH?

In his recent book, *From Scandal to Hope*, Fr. Benedict Groeschel, noted Franciscan preacher and psychologist, claims the sustained coverage of the scandals is a "media blitz" against the Church:

> We are experiencing a *media blitz* right now against the Catholic Church. Why? They seemed to be our friends only a short while ago. Now they have very good reasons to attack us. In the early 1990s, an opinion poll was conducted among media personnel in California. Over ninety percent of those involved in the media establishment were in favor of equating homosexual relationships with traditional marriage. Considerably more than ninety percent were in favor of abortion-on-demand. That's why they consider us their enemies.[24]

Father Groeschel later explains how, with society's eroticization, the problem of sexual abuse permeates every social institution: the family, the Armed Forces, schools, and youth organizations. This sexual-abuse problem, he says, is cross-denominational, with cases existing in every religion. Furthermore, the practice of settling sexual-abuse cases out-of-court and thereby avoiding the publicity inherent to court cases is also common to all denominations. Nevertheless, Father Groeschel says, when it comes to the Catholic Church the

24. Fr. Benedict J. Groeshel, C.F.R., *From Scandal to Hope* (Huntington, Ind.: Our Sunday Visitor Publishing Division, 2002), p. 45.

media made Her the target for a blitz—as if only the Church had sexual-abuse problems and made use of out-of-court settlements. Father Groeschel is careful to point out that the media's bias does not mean that bishops were not imprudent and did not make mistakes.

Father Groeschel proves his point by including a study by James O. Clifford as an appendix in his book. The study compares media handling of sexual abuse cases involving teachers and priests and shows a glaring disparity.[25]

PART OF THE PROBLEM, NOT THE SOLUTION

To conclude this analysis of the media's role in the present scandals, one must make several distinctions.

A horrendous crisis exists in the Church. Sexual scandals are a facet of this crisis. However, even more horrendous than such scandals is the loss of Faith and of priestly and religious identity.

On one hand, the crisis exists. Tackling it is another thing altogether.

In handling and solving this crisis, one must exercise great care. The crisis in the Church must be denounced in a way that will not impair the Faith of the common people. One must neither scandalize the faithful nor create a climate of revolt that might pave the way for those opportunists who love to fish in troubled waters and quickly become self-appointed "saviors."

The Church never feared the truth. As Pope Leo XIII says, quoting from the Scriptures: "God has no need of our lies."[26] The same Pontiff gives this norm: "Say nothing false, hold back nothing true."[27]

One must not close his eyes to scandal or try to justify the

25. Ibid. pp. 208-212.
26. Job 13:7. Encyclical *Depuis Le Jour*, Sept. 8, 1899 no. 25.
27. Brief *Saepe numero*, Aug. 28, 1883.

unjustifiable, but rather analyze everything in light of the Faith and Church history. The latter shows the countless crises the Divine Redeemer has allowed His Spouse to endure.[28]

If the current scandals are presented from a merely human standpoint without this supernatural perspective, and the Church is seen like any other earthly institution, the resulting naturalistic approach will distort the reporting. The media, incidentally, have largely adopted this approach.

The liberal media's role in the present crisis leaves little room for optimism. Its handling of the scandals is not part of the solution but part of the problem.

28. See the Introduction.

A/P Wide World Photo

Innocent victims of sexual abuse deserve sympathy and support, but personal tragedy cannot be used as pressure for structural changes in the Church. Survivors Network of those Abused by Priests (SNAP) leaders Mark Serrano and David Clohessy demonstrate at the Bishops' meeting in Dallas.

A/P Wide World Photo

Some of the alleged victims have strange stories. Arthur Austin (photo) is presented by SNAP as a "victim turned survivor." The VOTF calls him a "prophet." In an interview, he recounts how he was a homosexual young man of 20 when abused by Father Shanley.

CHAPTER 2

When Personal Tragedy Becomes Ideological Pressure

No one doubts that all innocent victims of sexual abuse (not only by members of the clergy) deserve sympathy and support, and that everything should be done to lessen their suffering and remedy their trauma.

However, this sympathy should not be diverted toward promoting a particular ideology nor should personal tragedy be used to exert moral and psychological pressure for revolutionary changes in the Church.

IDEOLOGICALLY MOTIVATED VICTIM GROUPS

Unfortunately, some victims' groups, such as Survivors Network of those Abused by Priests (SNAP) and the Coalition of Catholics and Survivors (CCS), took this course.

For example, Lee White, SNAP's Virginia director, declares: "There's a struggle over power going on. Lay people are asking for more of a voice in the Church, and bishops are digging in their heels. They see lay people as a threat to their authority and their power."[1]

This statement reflects an ideology similar to that of Marxist class struggle.

On the other hand, while raising very grave theological questions, Mr. White criticizes the very nature of the Church's structure.

Phil Saviano, SNAP's New England Regional Director, demonstrates a similar ideological stance in a speech delivered at Voice of the Faithful's first national convention in July.[2]

1. Susan Hogan Albach, "Some Bishops Leery of Sharing Authority," *The Dallas Morning News*, June 16, 2002.
2. www.survivorsnetwork.org/Actions_by_Parishoners/Phil_Saviano_speech.htm.

Mr. Saviano notes the irony of speaking before the Voice of the Faithful, since he qualifies himself as not faithful. "I was, once, but I lost my faith," he notes, "before I'd even gone through puberty."

The SNAP leader insinuates that being a victim gives him the authority to speak to the faithful and incite them to action. He further states that he shares common ground with Catholics in their questioning of the Faith.

Finally, he also presents the crisis in the Church as a power struggle. His words imply the following parallel: As various individuals became "victims" through sexual abuse, so also the laity became the "victim" of an abusive hierarchy. As the "victims" reclaim their dignity in becoming "survivors," so also the laity recovers its usurped authority in establishing a "democratic" Church. In Mr. Saviano's words:

> I began by referring to victims taking back their power. That's what you've got to do, too! Make the next 10 years count the most!
>
> You want to keep the faith? Fine. Just change this godforsaken church!
>
> Use your ears to listen to our experiences. Sure, we were once victims, but by finding the courage to speak out and change the world, we've become survivors, and we're worthy of your respect.

CREATING A CLIMATE OF INTENSE EMOTIONALISM

Speaking at VOTF's July 2002 convention, CCS activist Susan Renehan mentioned how she was abused by a priest and

cont. All quotations in the following paragraphs are from this transcript.

consequently left the Church. Her indicting words were brutal: "Priests are raping and abusing your children and your bishops are hiding it."[3]

The intense emotionalism at the convention facilitated the formulation of this abusive generalization, and it engendered, in its turn, new emotion. Ms. Renehan's words suggested that priests are attacking *all* children and *all* bishops are hiding the fact. The statement created a sense of urgency, calling for quick and energetic action.

"SURVIVOR" AS A "TALISMANIC" WORD

The word "survivor" is increasingly used to describe those who suffered sexual abuse. Father Doyle, for example, used the expression "victims turned survivors" in his keynote speech at VOTF's Boston convention. Nearly all the other speakers followed his lead. Throughout the day, the word rang out like a mantra in an apparent, intentional effort to make it sink in. No one at the convention explained why this word was chosen.

As cited earlier, SNAP leader Phil Saviano gives a confused definition of "survivor" as a person abused by the clergy who retakes the power stolen from him.

SNAP executive director David Clohessy has a different explanation of his organization's use of the word "survivor" in its title. He says:

> Unfortunately, some men and women do not survive childhood sexual abuse. While every victim's experience is tragic, the stories of those who commit

3. Eric Convey and Robin Washington, "Laity Gets Tough on Law," *The Boston Sunday Herald*, July 21, 2002. Cf. tape 02VF1, Resurrection Tapes, *Voice of the Faithful* National Conference.

> suicide as a result of abuse are among the most heart wrenching.... Many of us in the survivors movement consider ourselves fortunate to have endured our victimization and remained alive and sane. Some have not been so lucky.[4]

Thus, all those sexually abused who did not commit suicide would be "survivors." Using this logic, all who suffer broken engagements, job loss, or financial ruin and do not commit suicide can also be called "survivors" since some people do commit suicide because of such misfortunes.

Suffering sexual abuse is undoubtedly a traumatic experience. However, equating this with the experience of somebody who suffered immediate and serious risk of life, as in a serious accident or natural catastrophe in which others perished, is an exaggeration.

In this case, the exaggerated meaning attributed to the word becomes a means to exert psychological and emotional pressure.

"Survivor" becomes a "talismanic" word aimed at the ideological transshipment of the public. By careful spinning, a single word or expression that carries a world of ambiguous meanings can gradually influence and shape the thinking and mentality of the unwary.[5]

A STRANGE "VICTIM TURNED SURVIVOR"

One of the main "victims turned survivors" presented at the VOTF Boston convention was Arthur Austin. Why he is a

4. *SNAP BASICS Q & A with David Clohessy*, www.survivorsnetwork.org.
5. See Plinio Corrêa de Oliveira, *Unperceived Ideological Transshipment and Dialogue*, Chapter 3—"The Talismanic Words, a Stratagem of Unperceived Ideological Transshipment," *Crusade for a Christian Civilization*, Number 4, 1982. Currently available at www.tfp.org/what_we_think/dialogue/dialogue_chp3.html.

"victim" or "survivor" is not clear.

Writing on the Father Shanley scandal, *Boston Globe* reporter Sacha Pfeiffer touches on that of Arthur Austin, who has a claim pending against Father Shanley. Mr. Pfeiffer reports that Mr. Austin "went to the priest for counseling after his first gay relationship ended when he was 20. He was given 'access' to Shanley's body to ease the pain of the breakup, Austin said Shanley told him."[6]

Chuck Colbert writing in *National Catholic Reporter* says:

> ...two men, Arthur Austin of Braintree, Mass., and John Harris of Norwood, Mass., both of whom have accused Shanley of sexual abuse, are openly gay. During an interview, Mr. Austin said that as a young man of 20 he was facing a difficult time after the breakup of a same-sex relationship when Shanley took advantage of him.[7]

Mr. Austin also participated in CCS's march to the Boston Cathedral. Chuck Colbert writes: "Three openly gay men spoke out.... The third openly gay survivor to speak was Art Austin."[8]

How can Mr. Austin be presented as a "victim" or a "survivor" of homosexual abuse when he was himself an adult homosexual when he met Father Shanley?

VICTIMS AND SURVIVORS: NEW "PROPHETS?"

Nevertheless, SNAP's website calls Mr. Austin a "survivor"

6. "Famed 'Street Priest' Preyed Upon Boys," *The Boston Globe*, Jan. 31, 2002.
7. Chuck Colbert, "Documents Provoke Fresh Anger," *National Catholic Reporter*, Apr. 19, 2002.
8. Chuck Colbert, "Victims of Church Abuse Scandal Take to the Streets," innewsweekly.com, June 4, 2002.

and reproduces his April 8, 2002, remarks against Cardinal Law and the Catholic Church: "If the Catholic Church in America does not fit the definition of organized crime, then Americans seriously need to examine their concept of justice."[9]

"Survivor" Austin's opinion of the Church did not prevent Mary Scanlon Calcaterra from presenting him as a "prophet" at the VOTF convention.[10]

At the same convention, Susan Renehan presented the alleged victims almost as a new Magisterium of the Church when she addressed the audience: "You need our voice to teach you that you need to heal before you can forgive, and you need the truth before you can heal."[11]

Indicative of this intended shift in leadership and teaching authority was a sign carried by a CCS protester in front of Boston's Cathedral which read "The Victim is the Authority." Call to Action published a picture of the protest and the sign in its May 2002 issue of *Church Watch*.[12]

LINKS WITH REFORMIST GROUPS

The working links between these victims' groups and both old and new pressure groups pushing for Church reform also attest to their ideological motivation.

SNAP's website provides a link to Rent-A-Priest,[13] an association of married priests. For obvious reasons, this association advocates the end of priestly celibacy. It also defends the ordi-

9. www.peak.org/~snapper/Links_from_Home_Page/Art_Austin_statement.htm.
10. Eric Convey and Robin Washington, "Laity Gets Tough on Law."
11. Chuck Colbert, "4,000 Meet to Give Laity a Voice," *National Catholic Reporter*," Aug. 2, 2002. Cf. tape 02VF1, *Voice of the Faithful* National Conference.
12. www.cta-usa.org/watch05-02/watch05-02.html.
13. Helpful Links from SNAP, www.peak.org/Helpful_Links/Helpful_Links_Page.htm.
14. Cf. www.rentapriest.com, home page and especially the article "39 Popes Were Married," by married priest John Shuster, who defends the end of priestly

nation of women, the remarriage of divorced people, and democracy in the Church.[14]

SNAP and VOTF websites offer links to each other, and VOTF contributes financially to SNAP.

Call to Action's website offers links to SNAP and extensive and detailed instructions on how to get involved in the campaign. In the May 2002 issue of *Church Watch*, Call to Action features a picture of a Coalition of Concerned Catholics protest in front of Boston's Cathedral. Call to Action's caption reads: "Groups like Coalition of Concerned Catholics (pictured) and Voice of the Faithful in Boston are leading a revolution by lay people to take back the Church after failures of leadership by cardinals and bishops."[15]

On June 4, 2002, the same group, under its new name, Coalition of Catholics and Survivors (CCS) promoted a march to Boston's Holy Cross Cathedral. Chuck Colbert reported on the march:

> Lesbian and gay Catholics, along with more than 20 members of Dignity/Boston, the region's leading gay Catholic faith community, took part in this past weekend's solidarity walk and survivors' storytelling event. The solidarity walk was sponsored by the Coalition of Catholics and Survivors (CCS), one of two major church-reform and advocacy organizations that have sprung to life in the wake of the Boston archdiocese sex abuse scandal.[16]

OVERLAPPING MEMBERSHIPS

celibacy and the ordination of women. See also "The Church IS a Democracy," by Daniel C. Maguire, which, as the title of the article clearly implies, denies that the Church is a hierarchical society.

15. www.cta-usa.org/watch05-02/watch05-02.html.
16. Chuck Colbert, "Victims of Church Abuse Scandal Take to the Streets."

Chuck Colbert points out VOTF and CCS share a significant number of overlapping members.[17] Overlapping appears to extend to other victims' and reformist groups as well.

Reporting on the bishops' Dallas meeting, *The Boston Globe*'s Thomas Farragher cites a telling example: "[Cardinal Law] stopped briefly to speak with three members of the Coalition of Catholics and Survivors, Joseph E. Gallagher Jr. of Wellesley, Anne Barrett Doyle of Reading, and Janice Leary of Natick. Ms. Leary is also a member of the Wellesley-based Voice of the Faithful."[18]

Mr. Farragher could have added that Ms. Doyle, like Ms. Leary, is a member of VOTF's Lay Leadership Council,[19] and that Ms. Leary is deeply involved with Call to Action. An April 2002 article in *Call to Action News* says:

> CTA New England activists in the Boston region, coordinated by Jan Leary, *are at the heart of a concerned Catholics coalition* that will form a human chain around the cathedral for a prayer of solidarity with sexual abuse victims at 3 PM Good Friday. Their spring conference Apr. 14 in Belmont, Mass., will include a workshop on the church crisis led by [Mary Jo] Bane.[20]

In a testimonial as to why she joined VOTF, Janice Leary says:

> I identify myself as a "Call to Action Catholic": I

17. Chuck Colbert, "New Group Pushes for Change," *National Catholic Reporter*, Apr. 26, 2002.
18. Thomas Farragher, "Law Will Face Many Skeptics on His Return," *The Boston Globe*, June 16, 2002.
19. See www.votf.org/Who_We_Are/council.html
20. "Priest Pedophilia Scandal Awakens Catholics to Church Reform," *Call to Action News*, April 2002. Our emphasis.

> co-founded Mass Women Church, started the Call To Action/Massachusetts group,...started "Save Our Sacrament: Reform of Annulment and Respondent Support" and became a member of COR (Catholic Organizations for Renewal) a national umbrella group whose members represent all the major progressive Catholic organizations throughout the country.[21]

Janice Leary, as head of "Save Our Sacrament: Reform of Annulment and Respondent Support," is an official member of the international reformist group We Are Church.[22]

THE REFORMISTS' IDEOLOGY: A NEW LIBERATION THEOLOGY

In Latin America, proponents of liberation theology used the poor (dubbed the "oppressed") as a pretext for a class struggle that would liberate them from oppressive structures, meaning the capitalist system. The proposed solution was the Marxist classless society.

With the sexual scandals, a new class struggle is being created in the United States. The "oppressed" class consists of sexual abuse victims. The "oppressors" are clergymen and the hierarchical structure of the Church. The proposed solution is ending this clerical oppression by establishing a classless society in the Church.

---

21. Originally posted at www.voiceofthefaithful.org/whyijoined.html. It has now been removed.

22. See www.we-are-church.org/us/members.html. On July 10, 2002 the Communications Office of the Spanish Bishops' Conference issued a statement on We Are Church, affirming: "3—We Are Church advocates positions and beliefs that clearly remove it from the teachings of the Catholic Church, and are detrimental to ecclesial communion." Nota de la Oficina de Información de la Conferencia Episcopal Española Sobre la "Corriente 'Somos Iglesia,'" July 10, 2002.

Liberation theology in Latin America adopted the Marxist myth of turning the proletariat into a redeemer. Because it is exploited, the oppressed proletariat does not participate in the sins of the oppressors. Therefore, when the proletariat liberates itself from oppression, it also liberates the very oppressors from the chains of the structures of oppression.

This same mythology is being applied to the present scandals. The victim of sexual abuse, the "survivor," does not participate in the vices of the oppressive clerical system. He is thus qualified to be the "redeemer" so that when he "liberates" himself, he liberates his oppressors by destroying the structure of oppression, that is, the Church's hierarchical structure.

From all of this it is clear that SNAP and CCS base their action on an ideology similar to that of reform groups that want to democratize the Church.

CHAPTER 3

Pressure Groups Subvert the Church by Exploiting the Scandals

Groups of theologians and lay activists long committed to changing Church structures and fitting them into an egalitarian mold are exploiting both the sexual scandals and the unjustifiable attitude of many bishops. They propose reforms that subvert authority in the Church by transferring "power" to the laity.

FISHING IN MURKY WATERS

Voice of the Faithful (VOTF) is among those fishing in murky waters. Founder and first president, Dr. James Muller, a longtime pacifist militant, does not hide that VOTF's real goal is to impose reforms of an egalitarian bent on the Church.

"Pedophilia is only a symptom of a disease," he says. "The disease is absolute power." "We're going to…create a mechanism for democracy."[1] "We have to balance the power of the hierarchy with the power of the laity."[2]

DEMOCRATIZATION OF THE CHURCH

At VOTF's Boston convention, Dr. Muller projected slides illustrating his understanding of the crisis in the Church. He concluded that the most profound cause is centralized power with no voice of the faithful. American democracy is his model for the Church.[3]

1. Mary Rourke, "Staking Their Claim," *The Los Angeles Times*, Apr. 23, 2002.
2. Miriam Hill, "Catholic Group in Boston Sows Seeds of Revolution," *The Philadelphia Inquirer*, May 15, 2002.
3. Cf. VOTF Working Paper: *The Problem and Our Vision* by Jim Muller from www.voiceofthefaithful.org.

Prof. Leonard Swidler, another speaker, supports the idea of women priests and democratization of the Church. He has drafted a "Constitution of the Church" and has written a book on the subject. His constitution would have the Church governed by a general council elected by representatives of national churches. This general council would be co-chaired by a pope and a lay person for non-renewable ten-year terms.[4]

With this constitution, Prof. Swidler merely transposes the principles of secular democracy to the Church. He makes the faithful (the "people" in a secular democracy), the source of ecclesiastical power and gives them control of this power. At the convention, Prof. Swidler's workshop was called "Guidelines for Setting up a Parish (Diocesan) Constitution."[5]

According to *The Philadelphia Inquirer*, VOTF intends to hold a "Continental Congress" in Philadelphia in 2003 to adopt a Constitution for the Church.[6]

FATHER DOYLE'S RADICAL EGALITARIANISM

Fr. Thomas Doyle, a keynote speaker at the VOTF convention, also stated that sexual abuse was only a symptom of "a deeper disease: a deeper and much more pervasive and destructive malady—the fallacy of clericalism."[7]

He said that the first symptom of this disease of clericalism is the false notion that the clergy have a special mission to sanctify the laity and are thus above everybody else and deserve privileges. To much applause, Father Doyle concluded that the most "deadly symptom of all is the unbridled addiction

4. Cf. *Toward a Catholic Constitution* (New York: Crossroads Publishing Company, 1996). Also see www.arcc-catholic-rights.org/constitution.htm.
5. See "Response of the Faithful," Agenda, Voice of the Faithful Conference, July 20, 2002.
6. Miriam Hill, "Catholic Group in Boston Sows Seeds of Revolution."
7. See tape 02VF2, *Voice of the Faithful* National Conference. All quotations from Father Doyle are taken directly from the recording purchased at the VOTF event.

TFP Archive

Fr. Thomas Doyle, O.P., received VOTF's first "Priest of Integrity Award." He outlined the reformist agenda and stated unequivocally that the "medieval model" of a "monarchical Church" is in its death throes.

TFP Archive

Dr. James Muller, founder of VOTF, defended the total democratization of the Church, using the American system of government as a model. He recommended using financial pressure: "No more donations without representation."

TFP Archive

Thomas Arens, international president of We Are Church, defended abolishing distinctions between clergy and laity at VOTF's first national convention.

to power" and urged his audience "to help those addicted to power free themselves from these chains."

The way to liberate the bishops would be to dismantle the hierarchical Church and implement democracy. Father Doyle garnered intense applause from the audience when he delivered an address defending egalitarian reforms echoing the modernist doctrine that Pope Saint Pius X condemned.

Father Doyle affirmed that it was "the governmental system that has caused" the sexual abuses, which in turn calls for "a real change." The abuse by the bishops, he said, is sustained "by the myth that what is good for this small minority, an episcopal leadership, is good for all of us; the myth that the good of the Church is our good."

This Dominican priest thundered about how the bishops have taken away the power of the laity, especially the underprivileged, who actually should be the real authorities: "The most vital members of the Church are not those who wear elaborate robes and sit on the thrones of power, but the marginalized, the hurting, the rejected, the forgotten, and the voiceless. And today we're taking back what has been hijacked from us."[8]

Father Doyle claimed that the present crisis marks "the beginning of the death throes of the medieval monarchical model" of the Church. The hierarchical Church was a result of the "misinterpretation of Christ's gift of the keys to the kingdom to Saint Peter." This erroneous interpretation served "as the rationale for a hierarchical system which was later invested with all the trappings of monarchy." As a consequence, he continued, "we must challenge ourselves and everyone who is part of the Church to abandon the notion that the Church is a kingdom made up of a string of fiefdoms called dioceses."

8. Such statements are similar to concepts found in liberation theology, where the oppressed and the marginalized are considered the real messiahs and redeemers of mankind.

Doing this will allow the Church to return to "Christ's radical egalitarianism."

Father Doyle's (not Christ's) "radical egalitarianism" led him to invite the audience "to abandon the magical thinking that sustains the medieval paradigm" of the hierarchical Church. This magical thinking was based on the "magical notion of sacraments and magicians as priests and bishops who administer them."

FINANCIAL BLACKMAIL

Dr. Muller recommends the use of financial pressure: "No more donations without representation. We have to gain financial power in this Church. They say the laity are weak, but we are 99.9 percent of the Church and 100 percent of the money, and we now have a structure where we can exert that power."[9]

Voice of the Faithful's new president, Dr. James Post, declares that a "hierarchy that failed to protect our children cannot be trusted to exercise sole control over the property, money and fate of our church." He defends the right of the laity "to participate in the decision-making processes of each parish, each diocese and the whole Catholic Church."

He defines the terms of the group's dialogue with the bishops. "Let me be clear about the terms of this dialogue: We will not negotiate our right to exist. We will not negotiate our right to be heard. We will not negotiate our right to free speech as American Catholics."[10]

REFORM MOVEMENTS ABOUND

Besides married priests, members of Call to Action and We

9. Quoted in Michael Paulson, "Lay Catholics Issue Call to Transform Their Church," *Boston Sunday Globe*, July 21, 2002.
10. Quoted in Chuck Colbert, "4,000 Meet to Give Laity a Voice," *National Catholic Reporter*, Aug. 2, 2002.

Are Church also spoke. These groups have long advocated a complete reform of the Church, including women's priesthood and the end of priestly celibacy.

Call to Action's Jan Leary and Linda Pieczynski directed workshops.[11] Dan Daley, co-director and a founder of Call to Action remarked that "many of those at the gathering were members of Call to Action Massachusetts." He later affirmed "he had begun conversation with leaders of the new group about possible collaboration in the future."[12]

We Are Church was represented by its international president, Thomas Arens, who came from Germany. In his speech Mr. Arens declared emphatically, "We have to abolish the two-class system in our Church." Just as the Berlin Wall was torn down, Mr. Arens said, "we have to tear down the wall which separates the clergy from the laity."[13]

SEXUAL LIBERATION MOVEMENTS ARE PRESENT

Pictures show at least one of the participants wearing a T-shirt bearing the Dignity/Boston logo. This homosexual group does not reflect Catholic teaching.

Speaking on "What Parishioners and Parents Can Do to Create a Sexually Safe Parish" was none other than Debra Haffner, a non-Catholic sexologist notorious for opposing the traditional teaching of the Church.

Ms. Haffner is a former president of the ultra-liberal Sexuality Information and Education Council of the United

---

11. A Call to Action press release of March 8, 2002 reads: "'The Vatican is trying to deflect attention from the role of the U.S. bishops who created this current clergy sex abuse crisis. It has nothing to do with gay priests,' said Linda Pieczynski, spokesperson for Call to Action." See www.cta-usa.org/press/gaypriests.html.
12. Colbert, "4,000 Meet to Give Laity a Voice."
13. Eric Convey and Robin Washington, "Laity Gets Tough on Law." Cf. tape 02VF4, *Voice of the Faithful* National Conference.

States (SIECUS), which advocates same-sex marriage and gay-lesbian religious ministers.[14]

Another speaker at the convention was Michelle Dillon, author of *Debating Divorce: Moral Conflict in Ireland, Gay and Lesbian Catholics*, and *Catholic Identity: Balancing Reason, Faith, and Power*. All her books have a liberal and reformist bent.[15]

14. "Defying conservative sentiment, some 850 religious leaders are embracing a declaration that all faiths should bless same-sex couples and allow gay and lesbian ministers. It is sponsored by the Sexuality Information and Education Council of the United States, or SIECUS. 'For too long, the only voices in the public square on religion and sexuality have been the anti-sexuality pronouncements of the religious right,' SIECUS head Debra Haffner told the Associated Press" (www.tennessean.com/sii/00/02/20/bishopbar20.shtml).
15. Ms. Dillon explains her thinking: "In my recently published book [*Catholic Identity: Balancing Reason, Faith, and Power*], I take a sociology of culture approach to the production of Catholicism. Focusing on institutionally marginalized Catholics (gays/lesbians, feminist and pro-choice Catholics), I show that contrary to a hierarchical, top-down model of religious production, these Catholics are active interpreters, and thus relatively autonomous producers of Catholic doctrine." (Cf. www.people.virginia.edu/~bb3v/symbound/forum/forum8/vforum4.html.)

TFP Archive

Bishop Matthew Clark of Rochester, N.Y. speaks at the New Ways Ministry's 4th National Symposium, "A National Dialogue on Lesbian/Gay Issues and Catholicism," held in March 1997 in Pittsburgh. The Symposium's motto was "the Church teaching/ teaching the Church."

TFP Archive

On March 1, 1997, Rochester's Bishop Matthew Clark offered a special Mass in Sacred Heart Cathedral for homosexuals and lesbians.

CHAPTER 4

Is Sodomy No Longer a Sin?

The current sexual scandals among the clergy represent just the tip of an enormous iceberg. The seeping of the so-called homosexual culture into the Catholic world since the sixties has reached unimaginable proportions. It can be found among the clergy, religious orders, and congregations as well as in seminaries, colleges, and schools.

That homosexuality could exist on such a scale inside the Church, the very soul of purity and chastity, is simply tragic. Equally tragic is the unpardonable connivance of shepherds who allowed it to spread unchecked for decades instead of taking adequate measures to prevent this evil from gaining access to the fold.

A CONCERTED EFFORT TO DISASSOCIATE HOMOSEXUALITY FROM THE SCANDALS

Homosexuality is indeed the problem. The truth of the matter is that the vast majority of the exposed scandals are cases of homosexuality. Most cases are pederasty or ephebophilia, and thus a particularly heinous spillover of the more widespread problem of homosexuality.

Nevertheless, those in the homosexual movement realize the vital importance of laying the responsibility at another doorstep. "Pedophilia" and "sexual abuse" have become the expressions of choice. The latter term has a special advantage. With emphasis gradually shifting to "abuse," reformist groups pushing for democracy in the Church have begun ascribing responsibility for the sexual scandals to systemic abuse. In other words, the abuse is a product of the Church's hierarchical structure. Thus, sexual abuse is just the effect; the root cause is the "abuse of power."

Reformist groups blame the shepherds, but for the wrong reasons. Instead of charging them with failure to block the course of homosexuality over the decades, they are accused because their very episcopal office stands in the way of total license.

THE HOMOSEXUAL IDEOLOGY INFILTRATES THE CATHOLIC CHURCH

Twenty years ago, a Cuban-American priest, Fr. Enrique Rueda, published *The Homosexual Network.*[1] This comprehensive and well-documented study was a scathing indictment of the complicity of Catholic institutional leadership in the spread of the homosexual ideology in the United States.

Father Rueda details the efforts made by New Ways Ministry, Dignity, and the Catholic Coalition for Gay Civil Rights. He shows how the last group was linked to Call to Action,[2] which today supports Voice of the Faithful, Survivors Network for those Abused by Priests, and Coalition for Catholics and Survivors.

One example from Father Rueda's book illustrates the practical pastoral consequences of this homosexual infiltration in Catholic circles:

> The effects of the intellectual infiltration of the Catholic Church by the homosexual ideology are not merely theoretical, but strike at the very heart of Catholic life and tradition. An example of what the homosexual ideology can do to Catholic life is the case of the chaplain of Notre Dame University, one of the most prestigious Catholic institutions in the

1. Fr. Enrique T. Rueda, *The Homosexual Network: Private Lives and Public Policy.*
2. Ibid., p. 337.

> United States. In the February 1981 issue of *Notre Dame Magazine*, Father Robert Griffin, CSC, indicates that a young man came to confess to him that he was a homosexual and that he had been "unfaithful" to his regular sexual partner by having sex with another man. Father Griffin absolved him of his sin of "unfaithfulness."...
>
> It is significant that in the May 1981 issue of the magazine, two letters to the editor were reprinted in reply to Father Griffin's article. A letter from a priest was sympathetic to the prohomosexual position. Another letter, from a layman, correctly spelled out the traditional Catholic position.[3]

Father Rueda's wake-up call, being largely ignored, had no practical consequences and the homosexual movement continued its course.

Ten years later, on March 27-29, 1992, New Ways Ministry held a symposium in Chicago. Three bishops and about 600 people, mostly clergy and religious, attended the three-day event. The bishops in attendance were Bishop William Hughes of Covington, Ky., Bishop Kenneth Untener of Saginaw, Mich., and Detroit Auxiliary Bishop Thomas Gumbleton. *The Wanderer* published an extensive and detailed report on the event, but again, no effective action was taken against this example of homosexual infiltration of Catholic circles.

AN URGENT APPEAL TO OUR ECCLESIASTICAL AUTHORITIES

On March 1, 1997, Rochester Bishop Matthew Clark offered a special Mass in Sacred Heart Cathedral for homo-

3. Ibid., p. 335-336.

sexuals and lesbians. On March 7-9, New Ways Ministry held its 4th National Symposium in Pittsburgh. Bishops Clark and Gumbleton both spoke.

These two events led the American TFP to produce a paper titled "Is Sodomy No Longer a Sin? An Urgent Appeal to Our Ecclesiastical Authorities."[4] The document, published in *The Wanderer* on April 24, 1997, denounced the infiltration of "homosexual theology" in American ecclesiastical milieu. This infiltration is analogous to liberation theology so widespread in Latin America.

> Homosexual theology is a new liberation theology that uses the praxis of the 'lesbian/gay experience' to liberate man from the bonds of Christian morals.
>
> As Father Nugent and Sister Gramick, the co-founders of New Ways Ministry, boast, "Lesbian/gay theology is an example of authentic subversion. It involves a real turning from below with a scriptural analysis from the underside of society. Since God's spirit is continually revealing truth to the human heart, the scriptures contain some insights that can be made known to the Christian community only through the testimony of lesbian and gay people" (Robert Nugent and Jeannine Gramick, *Building Bridges* [Mystic, Conn.: Twenty-Third Publications, 1995], p. 190).

The TFP paper shows how Bishops Clark and Gumbleton lamented the Church's delay in changing Her position on homosexuality. Bishop Clark encouraged symposium participants, asking: "If individuals change quite slowly, how slow is institutional change?" Bishop Gumbleton added to this, say-

4. See Appendix A.

ing, "As Matthew [i.e. Bishop Clark] said, even if we are frustrated sometimes with the slowness of change, we still must put up with that frustration as we continue to struggle to make it happen."[5]

Bishop Gumbleton explained some points of homosexual theology quoting Andrew Sullivan, *Time*'s "Catholic homosexual" columnist: "...what is Andrew Sullivan telling us? He found God in his experience as a gay man. We know that God is love, and where there is love, there is God. And Andrew Sullivan tells us that his experience is that he finds God where he finds love."[6]

Quoting symposium speakers, including theologian Fr. Richard Peddicord, O.P., whose theories favor homosexuality, the TFP statement asks both the American bishops and the Vatican Congregation for the Doctrine of the Faith to take urgent measures to stop this homosexual infiltration in the Church.

Although the Vatican subsequently took some measures in the cases of Father Nugent and Sister Gramick, the spread of homosexual theology was never efficaciously barred.

DISCRIMINATION AGAINST MORALLY UPRIGHT SEMINARIANS

In his recent book, *Goodbye, Good Men: How Catholic Seminaries Turned Away Two Generations of Vocations From the Priesthood*,[7] investigative journalist Michael S. Rose describes in detail how the homosexual ideology devastated

5. Bishop Matthew Clark and Bishop Thomas Gumbleton, "Pastoral Care of Lesbian and Gay People," Plenary Session, New Ways Ministry 4th National Symposium, Pittsburgh, March 7-9, 1997.
6. Ibid.
7. Michael S. Rose, *Goodbye, Good Men: How Catholic Seminaries Turned Away Two Generations of Vocations From the Priesthood,* (Cincinnati: Aquinas Publishing Ltd., 2002).

many seminaries. The book's fourth chapter is titled "The Gay Subculture: How Homosexual Politics Discriminates Against Healthy, Heterosexual Seminarians."

In this chapter, Mr. Rose describes the paradoxical but true dominance of homosexual cliques in seminaries. He bases his affirmations on the testimony of priests and former seminarians.

A few quotations give a sufficient idea of what the book describes:

> "There was no discretion at all," he [Fr. John Trigilio] said of the gay subculture there. "The few times I was there, some of the seminarians would literally dress like gays from the Village. They would go so far as to wear pink silk...."
>
> "In my day at St. Mary's," said Father John Despard..."down the hall there would be two guys together in the shower and everybody knew it."[8]

The same Father Trigilio recounts his days in the Mary Immaculate Seminary, in Northampton, Penn., around 1984:

> We used to say, if you wore a cassock you were a reactionary "daughter of Trent." If you wore women's underwear, they make you seminarian of the year. We had a few guys who sometime wore women's clothing, lingerie, makeup, etc., and some who were as effeminate as could be. These were guys who were into all kinds of funny stuff. The campy ones at MIS [Mary Immaculate Seminary] would call each other by female names—like Mary, Sally, or Hazel—or use the feminine pronoun to refer to one another—she, her, etc. As is common in other seminaries, the

8. Ibid., p. 93.

> "ladies" at MIS would organize themselves, confident that the faculty was either ignorant, apathetic, or supportive of them.[9]

Testimonies published in Mr. Rose's book not only make it clear that homosexuality was tolerated and at times encouraged, but also prove that good seminarians who wanted to remain faithful to Church doctrine and morality were persecuted. These were often expelled or ostracized—to such an extent that many abandoned their vocation.

Fr. Joseph F. Wilson, commenting on Mr. Rose's book, says: "I and anyone who has been through the seminary in the last quarter century know [it] to be all too true. If anything, Mr. Rose was restrained."[10]

THE SEMINARIAN'S GREATEST OBSTACLE: THEIR OWN SPIRITUAL FATHERS

Writing on his own seminary experience, Father Wilson says:

> Discipline eroded, sexually scandalous situations proliferated, and good men abandoned their vocation in disgust. That vice rector left the priesthood…to "marry" the president of the Dallas Gay Alliance. He thoughtfully invited the seminarians to the festivities.
>
> He had been our moral theology professor (he had studied….at the local Methodist University). In his class we used Fr. Andre Guindon's texts, *The Sexual Language*.... I learned, for example that gay sex is in

9. Ibid., p. 242, (in Chapter 8, "The Vocational Inquisition: How the Orthodox Seminarian is Identified and Persecuted").
10. Joseph F. Wilson, "The Enemy Within: MTV is Not the Problem," in Paul Thigpen, Ed., *Shaken by Scandals* (Ann Arbor, Mich.: Servant Publications, 2002), p. 31.

> some ways preferable to straight sex because it is more innovative, expressive, playful....
>
> In my first year of theology...almost all our textbooks were paperbacks written by Protestants; our text on the Eucharist was written by a British Methodist.[11]

Father Wilson says that in the beginning of the eighties, the Holy See ordered an Apostolic Visitation of the seminaries: " It was carried out while I was still in seminary, and under our bishops it was rendered a toothless joke."[12]

Father Wilson's conclusion is tragic: "Enough, then, about the corrosive effects of secular culture on seminarians and young priests. *The biggest obstacle to their formation as priests after the heart of Jesus is their own fathers in God.*"[13]

11. Ibid., pp. 32-33.
12. Ibid., p. 33.
13. Ibid. (Our emphasis).

CHAPTER 5

Symptoms of a Profound Crisis of Faith

The outrage over both the sexual scandals and the complicity of members of the hierarchy is definitely morally justified. This makes a discussion of the causes all the more necessary.

A SIN THAT CRIES TO HEAVEN FOR VENGEANCE

The sin of homosexuality is extremely grave. Consequently, catechisms and other texts used to list it among the sins that "cry to Heaven for vengeance."[1]

The *Catechism of the Catholic Church* promulgated by John Paul II in 1992 reads: "Basing itself on Sacred Scripture, which presents homosexual acts as acts of grave depravity, tradition has always declared that 'homosexual acts are intrinsically disordered.'"[2]

Homosexuality is a sin condemned in the Old Testament,[3] by both Saint Peter and Saint Paul in the New Testament,[4] by Fathers and Doctors of the Church, and by the Popes for 2,000 years. Saint Peter Damian, a Doctor of the Church, says it "should not be considered an ordinary vice, for it surpasses all

1. "Since the sixteenth century, it has been the custom to apply the term 'sins that cry to heaven for vengeance' to certain faults that gravely violate the social order, and which Sacred Scripture expressly says cry to heaven for vengeance, i.e., call down God's punishment on those who commit them. There are four such sins: homicide (Gen. 4:10); *sodomy* (Gen. 10:13); oppression of widows and orphans (Exod. 22:22ff.); depriving workers of their just wage (Deut. 24:17ff.; James 5:4)." Dom Gregorio Manise, O.S.B., "Sins That Cry To Heaven For Vengeance," in *Dictionary of Moral Theology* (Westminster, Md.: The Newman Press, 1962), p. 1139. Our emphasis.
2. *Catechism of the Catholic Church*, 2nd ed., #2357.
3. Gen. 19:1-29; Lev. 18:22; Deut. 22:5.
4. 2 Pet. 2:6-7; Rom. 1:24-27; 1 Cor. 6:10; 1 Tim. 1:10.

of them in enormity."[5]

Saint Thomas Aquinas explains that since God made the natural order, violating this order by committing the sin of homosexuality insults the Creator. He quotes from Saint Augustine:

> Those foul offenses that are against nature should be everywhere and at all times detested and punished, such as were those of the people of Sodom, which should all nations commit, they should all stand guilty of the same crime, by the law of God which hath not so made men that they should so abuse one another. For even that very intercourse which should be between God and us is violated, when that same nature, of which He is the Author, is polluted by the perversity of lust.[6]

When a priest or a person consecrated to religious life commits this sin, it becomes a sacrilege.[7] When aggravated by child abuse, the Savior's terrible words apply: "It were better for him that a great millstone should be hanged about his neck, and that he be drowned in the depths of the sea."[8]

SINS AGAINST THE FAITH ARE CHASTISED WITH UNBRIDLED SENSUALITY

From a theological standpoint, God chastises those who abandon the Faith with unbridled sensuality.

5. St. Peter Damian, *Liber Gomorrhanius* (*Book of Gomorrah*) in Migne, *Patrologia Latina*, Vol. 145, col. 159-190.
6. St. Thomas Aquinas, *Summa Theologica*, II-II, q.154, a.12.
7. "*Carnal sacrilege*: a carnal act between two people at least one of whom is consecrated to God through the priesthood or through a public vow of chastity." Marcellinus Zalba, S.J., *Theologia Moralis Summa* (Madrid: Biblioteca de Autores Cristianos, 1957), Vol. II, p. 153.
8. Matt. 18:6; Mark 9:41; Luke 17:2.

The Roberti-Palazzini *Dictionary of Moral Theology* classifies homosexuality as one of the "sins that cry to heaven for vengeance."
"The Destruction of Sodom" by Gustave Doré

In his Epistle to the Romans, Saint Paul explains that the pagans, violating the Natural Law written on their hearts, exchanged the true God for idols and were consequently punished:

> Therefore, God handed them over to degrading passions. Their females exchanged natural relations for unnatural, and the males likewise gave up natural relations with females and burned with lust for one another. Males did shameful things with males and thus received in their own persons the due penalty for their perversity.[9]

The great exegete Cornelius a Lapide (1567-1637) comments on Saint Paul's teaching:

> Monstrous sensuality is a punishment for infidelity, impiety, and heresy. This is so because where faith is absent there is no grace of God, and where the grace of God is absent there can be no chastity but only concupiscence.... Heresy and infidelity are born from pride; and the punishment of pride is sensuality just as the prize for humility is chastity. This is the just order established by God; for if man subjects his mind to God, so will his body be subject as well. On the contrary, when man rebels against Him, so does his body rebel against him too, as Saint Gregory aptly puts it: "Humility guarantees the purity of chastity, for if one's spirit is piously submissive to God, one's flesh does not illicitly revolt" (*lib. XXVI Moral., XII*).[10]

9. Rom. 1:26-27.
10. Cornelii a Lapide, *Commentaria in Scripturam Sacram* (Paris: Vivès, 1863), Vol. 18, p. 54.

Analyzing Saint Paul's words in Romans 1:26-27, Jesuit Father Fernand Prat explains that the process of decadence has two phases: "first, the gradual clouding of the mind, and then the perversion of the heart and the obliteration of the moral sense."[11]

The present crisis shows how far the obliteration of the moral sense has reached in our days, even among the clergy.

THE ROOT OF THE SCANDALS: A CRISIS OF FAITH

Consequently, one must look for the most profound causes of the moral scandals shaking the Church in a crisis of Faith.

In his first encyclical, *E Supremi*, Pope Saint Pius X (1903-1914) alludes to this apostasy, saying:

> We were terrified beyond all else by the disastrous state of human society today. For who can fail to see that society is at the present time, more than in any past age, suffering from a terrible and deep-rooted malady which, developing every day and eating into its inmost being, is dragging it to destruction? You understand, Venerable Brethren, what this disease is—apostasy from God.[12]

Saint Pius X waged a relentless struggle against the modernist heresy that had deeply infiltrated the Church. He pointed out its errors and methods of action in a number of Pontifical documents and took many disciplinary measures.[13]

This heresy, nevertheless, carried on its insidious action inside the Church. Pius XII launched several important

11. Fernand Prat, S.J., *The Theology of Saint Paul* (Westminster, Md.: The Newman Bookshop, 1952), Vol. I, p. 201.
12. Pius X, *E Supremi*, Oct. 4, 1903, no. 2.
13. See Denzinger, nos. 2001-2176.

encyclicals against it.[14] Paul VI denounced its presence in the Encyclical *Ecclesiam Suam*, in 1964:

> Was not the phenomenon of modernism, for example, which still crops up in the various attempts at expressing what is foreign to the authentic nature of the Catholic religion, an episode of abuse exercised against the faithful and genuine expression of the doctrine and criterion of the Church of Christ by psychological and cultural forces of the profane world?[15]

Despite all these efforts, the crisis in the Church, and the consequent crisis in society, has worsened.

Prof. Plinio Corrêa de Oliveira observed:

> History narrates the innumerable dramas the Church has suffered in the twenty centuries of her existence: oppositions that germinated outside her and tried to destroy her from outside; malignancies that formed within her, were cut off by her, and thereafter ferociously tried to destroy her from outside.
>
> When, however, has history witnessed an attempted demolition of the Church like the present one? No longer undertaken by an adversary, it was termed a self-destruction in a most lofty pronouncement having world-wide repercussion.[16]

The "self-destruction" Prof. Corrêa de Oliveira refers to is drawn from a famous statement of Paul VI. On December 7, 1968, in an allocution to the students of the Pontifical Lombard

14. *Mystici Corporis Christi* (1943), *Mediator Dei* (1947), and *Humani Generis* (1950).
15. Paul VI, *Ecclesiam Suam*, Aug. 6, 1964, no. 26.
16. Plinio Corrêa de Oliveira, *Revolution and Counter-Revolution* (York, Penn.: The American Society for the Defense of Tradition Family and Property, 1993), p. 148.

Seminary, this Pontiff affirmed: "The Church finds herself in an hour of disquiet, of self-criticism, one might even say of *self-destruction*."[17]

A few years later, in the allocution "*Resistite fortes in fide*," the same Pontiff said: "The smoke of Satan has entered into the temple of God through some crack.... An adverse power has intervened. His name is the devil, the mysterious being to which Saint Peter also alludes in his Epistle."[18]

In 1981, John Paul II painted the condition of the Church in somber tones:

> One must be realistic and acknowledge with a deep and pained sentiment that a great part of today's Christians feel lost, confused, perplexed, and even disillusioned: *ideas contradicting the revealed and unchanging Truth have been spread far and wide; outright heresies in the dogmatic and moral fields have been disseminated, creating doubt, confusion, and rebellion; even the liturgy has been altered.* Immersed in intellectual and moral "relativism" and therefore in permissiveness, Christians are tempted by atheism, agnosticism, a vaguely moralistic illuminism, a sociological Christianity, without defined dogmas and without objective morality.[19]

Joseph Cardinal Ratzinger, Prefect of the Congregation for the Doctrine for the Faith, spoke in a similar fashion:

> Developments since the Council seem to be in

17. *Insegnamenti de Paolo VI*, Vol. 6, p. 188. Our emphasis.
18. Ibid., Vol. 10, pp. 707-709.
19. John Paul II, "Allocution to the Religious and Priests Participating in the First Italian National Congress on Missions to the People for the 80s," *L'Osservatore Romano*, Feb. 7, 1981. Our emphasis.

> striking contrast to the expectations of all, beginning with those of John XXIII and Paul VI … The Popes and the Council Fathers were expecting was a new Catholic unity, and instead one has encountered a dissension which—to use the words of Paul VI—seems to have passed over from self-criticism to self-destruction.[20]

Reflecting on the crisis of sexual scandals, one must conclude that the punishment of abandonment by God has fallen not only upon civil society but also large sectors of the Church darkened by the "smoke of Satan."

20. From Vittorio Messori, *The Ratzinger Report* (San Francisco: Ignatius Press, 1985), p. 29.

CHAPTER 6

The Bishops' Responsibility

Long years of misunderstood tolerance and neglect, and even the connivance of bishops in some cases, allowed the crisis to reach its present proportion.

The reformist "solution" is to tear down the hierarchical structure of the Church, stripping bishops of episcopal authority and "empowering" the laity. The reformists claim that the bishops, who are responsible for the crisis, are incapable of extricating the Church from it and must be held "accountable to the laity."

This is a false solution.

MISPLACED CONCERN WITH THE MEDIA

Unfortunately, the attitude of many bishops toward the cases of priestly pederasty seems conditioned more by the media's clamor than by the good of souls.

The meeting of the United States Conference of Catholic Bishops (USCCB) in Dallas was their first gathering since the media's massive campaign began in January. The faithful and the nation waited in great expectation for their words and actions on this momentous occasion. The media also waited, and to ensure the desired results, they came in overwhelming numbers.[1]

DALLAS: "RITUALS OF SELF-DENIGRATION"

The bishops' first meeting responding to this historic crisis

1. "Few of the national meetings the bishops hold twice a year have drawn more than a handful of journalists.... This bishops' meeting has drawn more than a thousand requests for news credentials. More than 750 reporters have received them, but others are protesting their exclusion." Laurie Goodstein, "Bishops Must Reassure Laity While Setting Policy on Abuse," *The New York Times*, June 9, 2002.

became a media circus. Fr. Richard John Neuhaus, the editor of *First Things*, describes it well:

> Dallas was a classic instance of what social scientists call the rituals of self-denigration. Almost three hundred bishops sat in mandatory docility as they were sternly reproached by knowing psychologists, angry spokespersons for millions of presumably angrier lay people, and, above all, by those whom the bishops learned to call, with almost cringing deference, the 'victim/survivors.' At times the meeting took on the appearance of a self-criticism session in a Maoist reeducation camp. But it was all in the good cause of finding a way to "move on," as it is said, from an undoubted catastrophe. It would be cynical to deny that there were signs of deep remorse, contrition, and penitence. There were. Even if it was a bit much to have reporters counting how many bishops shed tears as they listened to the victim/survivors. Tears earned a gold star and welling eyes an honorable mention from the media masters of the rites of self-denigration. Like schoolboys, the bishops anxiously awaited the evening news to find out their grades.[2]

Father Neuhaus further states that the bishops caved in to media pressure and avoided dealing with the problem of homosexuality among the clergy for fear of accusations of "homophobia" and headlines like "Bishops Mandate Witch-hunt Against Gays."[3]

2. Fr. Richard John Neuhaus, "Scandal Time III," *First Things*, June/July 2002.
3. Ibid.

THE NATIONAL REVIEW BOARD

In Dallas, the bishops tried to adjust to the pressure. With a vote of 239—13, they adopted the Charter for the Protection of Children and Young People. This Charter adds to the bureaucracy in USCCB's Washington offices and chips away at the bishops' authority in their own dioceses. It establishes an Office for Child and Youth Protection to audit compliance of bishops nationwide and a Review Board to inspect the work of the new Office.

Oklahoma Governor Frank Keating was chosen to head the Review Board by USCCB president Bishop Wilton Gregory. Other members include the pro-abortion Leon Panetta, chief of staff for former President Clinton.

Writing in *The New York Times*, Gov. Keating says he will answer to the laity, not to the bishops: "I envision the commission [the National Review Board] as apart from the conference of bishops, answering first of all to the laity we represent. We will coordinate with local parish and diocesan councils to ensure that the voice of the laity is heard."[4]

Gov. Keating intends to call the bishops to task:

> We have to participate in the restoration of faith to the faithful. And you can't do that by suggesting there is some person in this mix who is above corrective action.... The church needs a real thorough scrubbing. You will not see faint-heartedness in this process.[5]
>
> I agree with Cardinal Francis George of Chicago, who has said that the bishops must be held accountable for what has occurred—and what will occur—on

4. Frank Keating, "Trying to Restore a Faith," *The New York Times*, June 15, 2002.
5. Thomas C. Fox, "Watchdogs Needed to Restore Faith in Bishops," interview of Frank Keating, *National Catholic Reporter*, July 19, 2002.

A/P Wide World Photo

Creating a lay National Review Board to "control" the bishops directly opposes Church tradition and Her hierarchical nature. Board Chairman Gov. Frank Keating (center between Bishops Gregory and Galante) surprisingly affirmed that "Luther was right about lay involvement in reform."

> their watch. The commission will see to that.... The commission is capable of calling the public's attention to bishops who do not follow the guidelines adopted yesterday, and we intend to do so.[6]

Gov. Keating sees a theological side to his work and himself as a reformer: "The commission's third and most important goal might best be described as theological. We do not propose to rewrite church doctrine. But to undertake the reform of a religious institution."[7]

What Gov. Keating's reform might entail can only be surmised from his admiration for Martin Luther:

> Remember, it was Martin Luther who suggested early in his efforts that the lay community get involved in reforming the Church so there would not be a collapse of faith by the faithful.
>
> Unfortunately, in retrospective, Martin Luther was right. Just think what positively could have occurred if lay people in the sixteenth and fifteenth centuries had been involved. None of us is a theologian, and every one of us [on the board] recognizes the authority of those who speak for the religious part of the Church. But the human part needs more lay involvement, to make sure these types of calamities don't occur again.[8]

The creation of a lay supervisory board to "control" the bishops' actions on the sexual scandals directly opposes the whole of Church tradition and Her hierarchical nature as estab-

6. Keating, "Trying to Restore a Faith."
7. Ibid.
8. Wayne Laugesen, "Luther Was Right, Says Bishops' Point Man," interview of Frank Keating, *National Catholic Register*, June 30–July 6, 2002.

lished by Our Lord.

By Divine Law and canonical regulations, the bishops are entirely sovereign in their dioceses and depend solely on the Pope. They may not be summoned by other bishops or held accountable by the laity.[9]

IS A PLENARY COUNCIL THE SOLUTION?

Some well-intentioned bishops called for a plenary council. In normal times, this might be a solution. If Dallas, however, is any indicator, a plenary council might prove disastrous.

The following historic example might foster better understanding of the present situation.

In 1789, the French government desperately needed money to pay for past wars, including its support for the American Revolution. Despite these financial troubles, the 800-year-old Bourbon monarchy in France appeared to be a solid institution with no reason to fear for its existence. A handful of revolutionaries thought otherwise.

Jacques Necker, finance minister and a promoter of the "new ideas," proposed convening the Estates General. This was an ancient French institution that gathered representatives of the three estates: the clergy, the nobility, and the people. Its role was to authorize the king to take exceptional measures, such as the creation of new taxes.

Through crafty maneuvering, revolutionaries and partisans of the new ideas took advantage of the assembly to completely change its function and assist them in their designs. From a simple meeting to debate taxes, the Estates General was turned into a National Assembly, which later evolved into a Constitutional Assembly. Before it was over, the French

9. Canon 381 §1.; cf. Salaverri, *De Ecclesia Christi*, in VV.AA, *Sacrae Theologiae Summa*, Vol. I, nos. 356-370, pp. 625-630.

Revolution had guillotined France's king and queen, overthrown the Old Regime and its institutions, and brought fire and sword to France and Europe, soaking them in blood.

Confused situations, full of revolutionary agitation, call for exceptional leadership and resolute, courageous action tempered with great wisdom and prudence.

Today a plenary council gathering in a climate of confusion and agitation might well be hijacked by reformists and transformed into a constitutional assembly of sorts for the Church in America.

REFORM SOULS, DO NOT DESTROY THE CHURCH

The only true solution is returning to the Faith and reforming souls. If abandonment of the Faith is at the root of the problem,[10] then the solution is a return to the Faith.

Pope Adrian VI who reigned during the Renaissance and the Protestant Reformation, acknowledges the hierarchy's responsibility in times of great crises like his. He points out that healing must start where the disease began.

In a September 1, 1522, letter to the Imperial Diet of Nuremberg, the Pontiff writes:

> We frankly acknowledge that God permits this persecution of His Church [the Protestant Revolt] on account of the sins of men, and especially of prelates and clergy; of a surety the Lord's arm is not shortened that He cannot save us, but our sins separate us from Him, so that He does not hear. Holy Scripture declares aloud that the sins of the people are the outcome of the sins of the priesthood; therefore, as Chrysostom declares, when our Savior wished to

10. See Chapter 5.

> cleanse the city of Jerusalem of its sickness, He went first to the Temple to punish the sins of the priests before those of others, like a good physician who heals a disease at its roots. We know well that for many years things deserving of abhorrence have gathered round the Holy See; sacred things have been misused, ordinances transgressed, so that in everything there has been a change for the worse. Thus it is not surprising that the malady has crept down from the head to the members, from the Popes to the hierarchy.
>
> We all, prelates and clergy, have gone astray from the right way, and for long there is none that has done good; no, not one.... Therefore, in our name, give promises that we shall use all diligence to reform before all things the Roman Curia, whence, perhaps, all these evils have had their origin; thus healing will begin at the source of sickness.[11]

Everyone, both clergy and laity alike, must beseech God to send this true conversion.

11. Ludwig Pastor, *History of the Popes* (St. Louis: Herder, 1923), Vol. IX, pp. 134-135.

Chapter 7

The Church Is Holy Despite Having Sinners Within Her Fold

In the Nicene Creed, the faithful profess: "*Credo in unam,* sanctam, *catholicam et apostolicam Ecclesiam*"—"I believe in One, *Holy*, Catholic and Apostolic Church."[1]

When reciting the Creed, Catholics profess, therefore, to believe in the sanctity of the Church. This sanctity, nonetheless, is often not visible, especially when the weaknesses of Her members appear to demonstrate the opposite.

IS A SINNER LINKED TO THE CHURCH?

How can one explain that the sin of a member of the Church does not affect Her? The answer lies in the twofold reality of the Church, both supernatural and natural, divine and human.

The visible human element is subject to the effects of both Original Sin and the state of trial on this earth. This human element of the Church is subject to sin, even when vested in the priesthood or the loftiest dignities of the hierarchy.

However, there is an important distinction. When a member of the Church sins, he does not sin as a member of the Church or because of the Church. He sins because he is unfaithful to Her principles and to the life of grace She generated in him. Even in this state of sin, a member of the Church in one sense continues to be holy. He is holy because a holy sign, Baptism, links him to the Church and because the Church gives him the

1. These four attributes or characteristics (traditionally called "marks" of the Church)—her *Unity, Sanctity, Catholicity,* and *Apostolicity*—were introduced in the Nicene Creed at the Council of Constantinople (381 A.D.). These marks, the Council declared, distinguish the true Church of Christ from all other societies that claim this title and prove that She alone is the depository of the blessings of Redemption and the sole way to salvation that God offers to man (Cf. William H.W. Fanning, s.v. "The Church," in *Catholic Encyclopedia* [1913], Vol. III, pp. 758-760).

principles of truth and holiness contained in Her doctrine, morals, and sacraments.

A sinner is, therefore, a *bad member* of the Church, who diverges from Her by sinning; it is a partial divergence as long as he retains the Faith. He is an unhealthy member of the Church—like a tumor in a living body, to use Saint Augustine's realistic comparison.

Though he is a wilted branch attached to the vine, the sinner nevertheless preserves in himself some elements of holiness. In him, this holiness is the part belonging to the Church and it sustains him as a member of Her. The sin, which separates him from Her, makes him a son of the devil, in Saint John's strong words.[2]

THE CHURCH ENCOMPASSES SINNERS BUT NOT SIN

Charles Cardinal Journet provides this beautiful explanation:

> The Church contains sinners. But she does not contain sin. It is only in virtue of what remains pure and holy in them that sinners belong to her—that is to say in virtue of the sacramental characters of Baptism and Confirmation, and of the theological habits of faith and hope if they still have them. That is the part of their being by which they still cleave to the Church and are still within her. But in virtue of the mortal sin which has found its way into them and fills their hearts, they belong chiefly to the world and to the devil. "He who commits sin is of the devil" (1 John 3:8).
>
> Thus, the frontier of the Church passes through each one of those who call themselves her members,

2. 1 John 3:8-10.

TFP Archive

Saint Paul teaches that Christ immolated Himself for His Church, thus guaranteeing a "glorious Church, not having spot or wrinkle, or any such thing; but that it should be holy, and without blemish" (Eph. 5:25-27)

> enclosing within her bounds all that is pure and holy, leaving outside all that is sin and stain.... So that even here below, in the days of her pilgrimage, in the midst of the evil and sin at war in each one of her children, the Church herself remains immaculate; and we can apply to her quite fully and without any restriction the passage of the Epistle to the Ephesians (5:25-28)[3]

Therefore, although sin is often present in the human element of the Church, it does not affect the Church Herself. She continues as an adequate means of salvation given by Our Lord Jesus and animated and vivified by the Holy Spirit.

Regardless of how blatant and shocking the scandal is, and no matter how hard Her external and internal adversaries strive to use it to destroy Her, the Church walks forward serenely on Her way through this world, confiding in Our Lord's words to the Apostles after the Resurrection: "Behold I am with you all days, even to the consummation of the world."[4]

THE HOLINESS OF CHRIST'S CHURCH

Fr. Auguste-Alexis Goupil, S.J., keenly observes that sanctity in the Church is not measured with statistics. For the Church to be holy, all Her members do not have to be perfect. Because of human weakness and man's moral liberty, which God respects, such perfection is impossible.

Furthermore, he explains, the existence of a large number of sinners proves nothing against the sanctity of the Church; for just as a stone naturally rolls down to the abyss, so also man, because of Original Sin, tends to let himself be carried away by sin. The existence of eminent saints—even though not as

3. Charles Cardinal Journet, *The Church of the Word Incarnate*, Vol. I, p. xxvii.
4. Matt. 28:20.

numerous as sinners—is a striking proof of the sanctity of the Church. Indeed, for these few to rise to the pinnacles of virtue, a powerful force must have come to their aid.[5]

The Church's sanctity derives from Her principles, sacraments, and hierarchy as established by Our Lord.

Fr. Christian Pesch, S.J., sums it up quite well:

> Christ established the Church holy, that is, to sanctify men (John 7; Eph. 5:26-27; Titus 2:14), and for this end He gave Her internal and external means of sanctification: a holy doctrine, holy precepts, holy government, holy sacraments. Now then, "every good tree bringeth forth good fruit" (Matt. 7:17), especially when it comes to supernatural and divine virtues. Therefore, there will always be holy men in the Church and not only with common sanctity but also with outstanding sanctity. *Otherwise Christ's prayer "that they also be sanctified in truth"* (John 17:19) *would be to no avail.* Nor will there be a lack of those who follow the evangelical maxims (Matt. 19:12, 21; 1 Cor. 7:25). Nor will signs of charismatic holiness [miracles], which Christ promised, cease to exist in the Church (Mark 16:17; John 17:22; 1 Cor. 12).[6]

Saint Paul proclaims the sanctity of the Church and says that Christ's love and immolation on Her behalf is the cause of Her sanctity:

> Christ also loved the church, and delivered Himself up for it; That He might sanctify it, cleansing it by laver

5. Fr. Auguste-Alexis Goupil, S.J., *L'Église* (Laval, France: Imprimerie-Librairie Goupil, 1946), pp. 27-28.
6. Fr. Christian Pesch, S.J., *De Ecclesia Christi*, in *Compendium Theologiae Dogmaticae* (St. Louis: Herder, 1913), Vol. 1, p. 172. Our emphasis.

> of water in the word of life: That He might present it to Himself as a glorious church, not having spot or wrinkle, or any such thing; but that it should be holy, and without blemish.[7]

THE CHURCH'S MYSTERIOUS PASSION

What can be said, on the other hand, about the self-destructive conduct of so many bishops?

No situation can be more tragic than this mysterious swooning of the hierarchy, a phenomenon so noted and commented on by eminent and learned people over the last thirty years.[8] The words of an eminent French theologian, Fr. Joseph de Sainte-Marie, O.C.D., are particularly opportune:

> We must be faithful to the Church even when Her hierarchy, through a mysterious divine permission, is failing so dramatically. Her infallibility is by no means in doubt, nor is the promise of Christ that "the gates of Hell shall not prevail against Her." However, this promise does not mean there will not be times of darkness. If the Son of God Himself endured death and the sepulcher, how would His Spouse not be called to undergo a similar or rather analogous trial?... What mysterious trials of annihilation still await Her? We cannot know what they will be in detail, but what we can know with certainty is that these trials will come. And we can even say they have already started.[9]

7. Eph. 5:25-27.
8. See statements in Chapter 5.
9. Fr. Joseph de Sainte-Marie, O.C.D., "Réfléxions Sur le Problème de la Messe Aujourd'hui dans l'Eglise," in *La Pensée Catholique*, July—Aug. 1974, pp. 25-27.

Chapter 8

The Church Is Hierarchical by Divine Institution

The defense of egalitarianism in the socio-political order is a philosophical error. When attempts are made to apply this egalitarianism to the Church, it becomes a theological error.

It is a theological error because Scripture clearly shows that Our Lord instituted a hierarchy to govern His Church. It is additionally erroneous because egalitarian efforts to abolish the distinctions between laity and clergy lead to an implicit denial of the sacrament of Holy Orders.

The learned Jesuit Fr. Joachim Salaverri says: "Christ gave the Apostles the authority to govern, teach, and sanctify, to which all must be subjected. He is, therefore, the author of the hierarchical society that is called the Church."[1]

The theologian Fr. Adrien Gréa explains: "The first foundation, the very core of hierarchical authority, is the sacrament of Holy Orders."[2]

A MATTER OF FAITH

In his book *Fundamentals of Catholic Dogma*, Dr. Ludwig Ott declares: "Christ gave His Church a hierarchical constitution." This is a proposition of faith. Thus, it cannot be denied without falling into heresy.[3]

The Council of Trent declares that those who deny the existence of a hierarchical priesthood or its power to consecrate, as well as those who affirm that "in the Catholic Church a hierar-

1. Salaverri, *De Ecclesia Christi*, in VV.AA, *Sacrae Theologiae Summa*, Vol. I, p. 543.
2. Fr. Adrien Gréa, *De L' Église et de Sa Divine Constitution* (Brussels: Société Génerale de Librarie Catholique, 1885), p.100.
3. Ludwig Ott, *Fundamentals of Catholic Dogma*, (Rockford, Ill.: TAN Books and Publishers, Inc., 1974), p. 276.

chy has not been instituted by divine ordinance, which consists of the bishops, priests, and ministers" be anathema.[4]

OUR LORD ESTABLISHED THE *CHURCH TEACHING* AND THE *CHURCH LEARNING*

Our Lord Jesus Christ Himself permanently established the hierarchical structure of the Church. Transforming and leveling this structure would thus alter Her very nature.

Our Lord wills that the Church be formed of two sectors: the "Church teaching" (*Ecclesia docens*) and the "Church learning" (*Ecclesia discens*). These two are complementary but are not equal.

The Church teaching consists of the Pope and the bishops. Their mission is to teach, govern, and sanctify the faithful. The Church learning consists of priests, religious and laity who must be taught, guided, and sanctified.[5]

This division is based on the mission received from the

4. Denzinger, no. 966.
5. The Church has two hierarchies by *divine institution*: the *Hierarchy of Order*, and the *Hierarchy of Jurisdiction*. The first is focused on the sanctification of souls through the celebration of the Mass and the administration of the Sacraments. To it belong bishops, priests, and deacons. The second is focused on governing the faithful toward salvation by an authoritative teaching of the Faith, the promulgation of laws, the issuing of legal judgments, and the application of canonical penalties (powers to teach, legislate, judge, and enforce); to this *Hierarchy of Jurisdiction* belong the Pope and the bishops in the external forum and authorized confessors exclusively in the internal forum. (Cf. *s.v. Ecclesia docens, Ecclesia discens*, and "Hierarchy" in Parente, Piolanti, and Garofalo, *Dictionary of Dogmatic Theology*, pp. 83, 124-125; Salaverri, *De Ecclesia Christi*, in VV.AA, *Sacrae Theologiae Summa*, Vol. I, no. 344).

   There is also a third hierarchy called the Hierarchy of Honor, *established by the Church Herself*. This hierarchy is made up by all ecclesiastical dignitaries according to the precedence and liturgical honors to which they are entitled. At the head of this hierarchy is, evidently, the Pope, who in addition to the primacy of jurisdiction also holds the primacy of honor. The Pope is followed by the cardinals, patriarchs, archbishops, primates, bishops, monsignors, canons, and other dignitaries, both in the Latin and Eastern rites.

Savior and the plenitude of the Sacrament of Holy Orders, that is, episcopal consecration. It does not depend on knowledge or sanctity. A simple priest, nun, or lay person may be more cultured or holier than a bishop, but continues to be part of the Church learning. Such, for example, was the case of Saint Bernard, Abbot of Clairvaux. His moral authority in the Church decisively resolved the most intricate ecclesiastical problems of the day, but it was a moral authority, not an authority of jurisdiction.

Through their sacramental consecration and union with the Pope, bishops are made successors of the Apostles and receive, together with the sacramental and jurisdictional authority, the charisms and graces necessary to exercise their office. Either they are faithful or unfaithful to these graces, and thus become bishops in the image of the Good Shepherd or in the image of the Hireling.[6]

In times of great spiritual crises, many bishops are unfaithful to these graces. God can allow this as a chastisement for the priests and laity. Nevertheless, a bishop's lack of fidelity does not entail automatic removal from office. Even in the case of manifest heresy and schism, such removal is effected only by a declaratory act of the competent authority, namely, the Holy See.[7] When subject to such dire conditions, the faithful must obey the bishop in everything that is for the good of the Church and the salvation of souls. They must resist, however, a bishop's command to do evil.[8] In such painful circumstances, and within stipulated conditions, the faithful always have the right (and at times the duty) of voicing their concern to the shepherds, and apprising the other faithful as to their opinion.[9]

6. See the Introduction.
7. Canon 194 (1983 Code); Canon 2314, § 1 (1917 Code).
8. St. Thomas Aquinas states: "If the faith were endangered, a subject ought to rebuke his prelate even publicly." *Summa Theologica*, II-II, q. 33, a. 4, ad 2.
9. Cf. Canon 212, § 3.

GOVERNMENT IN CIVIL SOCIETY HAS SEVERAL LEGITIMATE FORMS

In order to better understand Catholic doctrine on the form of government Our Lord established for the Church, it is useful to recall Church teaching on the forms of government in general.

Catholic Social Doctrine—and wholesome philosophy as well—teaches that there are three classical forms of government, all of which are legitimate and in accordance with natural order: monarchy, aristocracy, and democracy.

Saint Thomas Aquinas reasons that monarchy is the best form of government because it ensures peace: "The best government of a multitude is rule by one, and this is clear from the purpose of government, which is peace; for the peace and unity of his subjects are the purpose of the one who rules, and one is a better constituted cause of unity than many."[10]

Nevertheless, the Angelic Doctor concludes that monarchy tempered with elements of aristocracy and democracy is the best form of government for fulfilling man's needs.[11]

THE ORGANIC MONARCHY OF THE MIDDLE AGES

This tempered or mixed form corresponds to the organic monarchy of the Middle Ages, particularly in the thirteenth century during the reigns of Saints Louis IX of France and Ferdinand of Castile.

Referring to this period in the history of Christendom, Pope

10. St. Thomas Aquinas, *Summa Contra Gentiles*, (Garden City, N.Y.: Image Books, 1960), Book IV, p. 291. This is the common thought of Catholic authors and is taught by the Popes. See Plinio Corrêa de Oliveira, *Nobility and Analogous Traditional Elites in the Allocutions of Pius XII* (York, Penn.: The American TFP, 1993), Appendix IV, pp. 391-418.
11. Cf. St. Thomas Aquinas, *On the Governance of Rulers*, Gerald Phelan, trans. (Toronto: St. Michael's College Philosophy Texts, 1935), pp. 37-39.

Leo XIII writes:

> There was a time when the philosophy of the Gospel governed the States. In that epoch, the influence of Christian wisdom and its divine virtue permeated the laws, institutions, and customs of the people, all categories, and all relations of civil society. Then the religion instituted by Jesus Christ, solidly established in the degree of dignity due it, flourished everywhere, thanks to the favor of princes and the legitimate protection of magistrates. Then the Priesthood and the Empire were united in a happy concord and by the friendly exchange of good offices. So organized, civil society gave fruits superior to all expectations, whose memory subsists and will subsist, registered as it is in innumerable documents that no artifice of the adversaries can destroy or obscure.[12]

ATHEISTIC CONCEPT OF AUTHORITY: "POWER COMES FROM THE PEOPLE"

While Church doctrine accepts democracy as a legitimate form of government, the Popes nevertheless repeatedly condemn certain errors that have become increasingly associated with the concept, especially since the French Revolution.

In the eighteenth century, the so-called philosophers helped cause great social and political upheaval in France by spreading "new ideas." Rousseau, for example, advanced the notion that authority originates in the people. The people then delegate their authority to the ruler and can revoke it whenever they so chose.

In his encyclical *Diuturnum Illud* of June 29, 1881, Pope

12. Leo XIII, Encyclical *Immortale Dei*, no. 21.

Leo XIII rejects this theory and categorically affirms:

> Indeed, very many men of more recent times, walking in the footsteps of those who in a former age assumed to themselves the name of philosophers, say that all power comes from the people; so that those who exercise it in the State do so not as their own, but as delegated to them by the people, and that, by this rule, it can be revoked by the will of the very people by whom it was delegated. But from these, Catholics dissent, who affirm that the right to rule is from God, as from a natural and necessary principle.[13]

The same Pontiff also teaches that even when the people choose their ruler they do not confer authority on him, since authority comes from God: "And by this choice, in truth, the ruler is designated, but the rights of ruling are not thereby conferred. Nor is the authority delegated to him, but the person by whom it is to be exercised is determined upon."[14]

The Pontiff presents numerous quotations from both the Old and New Testaments, as well as texts from the Fathers of the Church, to confirm the doctrine on the divine origin of authority.[15]

EGALITARIAN CONCEPT OF DEMOCRACY

Besides combating this error on the origin of governmental authority, the Popes also fight the underlying egalitarianism.

Leo XIII's successor, Saint Pius X, condemns the false teaching of the French movement *Le Sillon* that democracy is

13. Leo XIII, Encyclical *Diuturnum Illud*, in Joseph Husslein, S.J., Ed., *Social Wellsprings: Fourteen Epochal Documents by Pope Leo XIII* (Milwaukee: Bruce Publishing Co., 1940), p. 50.
14. Ibid., p. 51.
15. Ibid., pp. 51-52.

the only legitimate form of government, since the other two are based on inequality and, therefore, injustice. The Pontiff says:

> The *Sillon*,...therefore, sows amongst your Catholic youth erroneous and fatal notions upon authority, liberty and obedience. The same is to be said with regard to justice and equality. It strives, it says, to attain an era of equality, which, owing to that fact alone, would be an era of greater justice. Thus to it every inequality of condition is an injustice, or at least a diminution of justice! A principle supremely contrary to the nature of things, productive of envy and injustice and subversive of all social order. Thus democracy alone will inaugurate the reign of perfect justice! Is it not an insult to other forms of government, which are thus degraded to the rank of wretched incapables? Moreover, the *Sillon* goes contrary to this point in the teaching of Leo XIII.... Therefore, in teaching that justice is compatible with the three forms of government referred to, it [Leo XIII's Encyclical *Au Milieu des Sollicitudes*] taught that in this respect democracy does not enjoy a special privilege. The Sillonists who contend to the contrary either refuse to hear the Church or form to themselves a conception which is not Catholic with regard to justice and equality.[16]

In his Christmas message of 1944, Pius XII condemns egalitarianism and makes the celebrated distinction between the *people* and the *masses*.

> In a people worthy of the name all inequalities

16. Pius X, Apostolic Letter *Notre Charge Apostolique*, in *American Catholic Quarterly Review*, Oct. 1910, pp. 700-701.

> based not on whim but on the nature of things, inequalities of culture, possessions, social standing—without, of course, prejudice to justice and mutual charity—do not constitute any obstacle to the existence and the prevalence of a true spirit of union and fraternity.
>
> On the contrary, far from impairing civil equality in any way, they give it its true meaning: namely, that before the state everyone has the right to live honorably his own personal life in the place and under the conditions in which the designs and dispositions of Providence have placed him.[17]

"DEMOCRACY" AS AN ANTONYM TO TOTALITARIANISM

It is also important to note another misuse of the word *democracy*.

The rise of dictatorships in Europe in the 1930s popularized a tendency which already existed in the nineteenth century to use the noun *democracy* as a synonym of *liberty* and an antonym of *totalitarianism*. This tendency became more firmly established during the Cold War to the point that even Popes have occasionally used the word in this broader sense, as opposed to its limited technical meaning designating a form of government.

According to Pius XII, the word *democracy*, used in this broad sense, "admits the various forms [of government] and can be realized in monarchies as well as republics."[18] The Pontiff also says: "With its pleiad of flourishing democratic communities, the Christian Middle Ages, particularly imbued with the spirit of the Church, showed that the Christian Faith

17. Vincent A. Yzermans, ed., *The Major Addresses of Pope Pius XII* (St. Paul: North Central Publishing Co., 1961), Vol. 2, pp. 81-82.
18. Ibid., pp. 80, 82.

knows how to create a true and proper democracy."[19]

This broadening of the meaning of democracy can cause confusion. Failure to distinguish between the two uses of the word can lead one inadvertently to the condemned Sillonist position that democracy is the only form of government synonymous with liberty.

Hence the emergence of a certain wariness about and even rejection of the other legitimate forms of government. Monarchy and aristocracy are seen as regimes lacking liberty. The conceptual distortion of democracy is dangerous since it obstructs people's understanding of the Church's own form of government and predisposes them to accept the reformists' clamors for a "democratic" Church as a legitimate alternative option.

THE CHURCH IS A MONARCHY BY THE WILL OF OUR LORD

Having thus recalled Church teaching on the forms of government and the condemned modern errors related to democracy, the Church's form of government must now be analyzed.

In his book *On the Roman Pontiff*, in the chapter titled "The Ecclesiastical Hierarchy, Monarchy of the Roman Pontiff,"[20] Saint Robert Bellarmine lambastes the Protestants who, by rejecting the Primacy of Saint Peter and the Sacrament of Holy Orders, deny the Church's hierarchical and monarchic nature.

Saint Robert Bellarmine analyzes the forms of government as such, weighing their advantages and disadvantages, and

19. Pius XII, "Inaugurazione dell'Anno Giuridico della Sacra Romana Rota," in *Discorsi e Radiomessaggi di Sua Santità Pio XII* (Vatican: Tipografia Poliglota Vaticana, 1964), Vol. VII, p. 206.

20. St. Robert Bellarmine, in *Bellarmine Extracts on Politics and Government from the Supreme Pontiff from Third General Controversy*, George Albert Moore, Trans., Ed. (Chevy Chase, Md: The Country Dollar Press, undated).

concludes that the best one in thesis is monarchy. He then goes on to ask what form of government—aristocratic, democratic, or monarchic—would be most fitting for the Church.

After careful analysis, based on the Scriptures and Doctors of the Church, he concludes that it is monarchy:

> If monarchy is the best and most excellent government, as above we have shown, and it is certain that the Church of God, instituted by the most sapient prince Christ, ought to [be] best governed, who can deny that the government of it ought to be a monarchy?[21]

Following Saint Robert Bellarmine, Fr. Christian Pesch affirms the common teaching of theologians: "The society established by Christ is a monarchic society."[22]

THE CHURCH IS A "FULL AND PERFECT MONARCHY"

If the Church has a monarchical form of government, it is important to know what kind of monarchy. Is it an absolute monarchy? A constitutional monarchy? A tempered monarchy like the organic monarchy of the Middle Ages?

Louis Cardinal Billot, S.J., makes a masterful analysis of this important issue. Following established custom, he first examines the forms of government as such according to the thought of Saint Thomas Aquinas, Saint Robert Bellarmine, Fr.

21. Ibid., p. 37.
22. Christian Pesch, S. J., "*De Ecclesia Christi*" in *Compendium Theologiae Dogmaticae*, Vol. I, p. 141. Cf. J.M. Hervé, *Manuale Theologiae Dogmaticae* (Paris: Berche et Pagis, Editores, 1952), Vol. I, pp. 306, 336, 345; L. Lercher, S.J., *Institutiones Theologiae Dogmaticae* (Barcelona: Herder, 1945), Vol. I, p. 163; also, Journet, *The Church of the Word Incarnate*, Vol. I, pp. 422-423.

Francisco Suárez, S.J., and other Scholastics, and then compares them to the Church's form of government.

In passing, Cardinal Billot analyzes the "divine right of kings" theory and distinguishes it from the Church's form of government. This theory maintained that God directly designates the sovereign, as happened in the Old Testament, and that kings, therefore, are answerable to Him alone.[23]

The "divine right of kings" was totally refuted by Catholic Doctors, especially Saint Robert Bellarmine and Suárez. These Doctors (whose doctrine was endorsed by the Popes) argue that while all authority comes from God, He does not directly designate either the holder of this authority or the temporal sphere's form of government. This is left to historical circumstances and custom.

Nonetheless, says Cardinal Billot, while this is true in the temporal political sphere, that is, in societies derived from the natural order, it is not true for the Church, a society of divine origin. Indeed, he states that the Church was not born from the bottom up like civil society but was founded from the top down, directly by Our Lord Jesus Christ, Who established Her definitive form.

The scholarly Cardinal explains:

> For authority [in the Church] comes directly from God through Christ, and from Christ to his Vicar, and from the Vicar of Christ it descends to the remaining prelates without the intervention of any other physical or moral person."[24]

Continuing his analysis, Cardinal Billot distinguishes the

23. This theory was adopted by certain Protestant rulers. In England, for example, it was adopted particularly by James I and his son, Charles I.
24. Louis Cardinal Billot, S.J., *Tractatus De Ecclesia Christi* (Rome: Aedes Universitatis Gregorianae, 1927), Vol. 1. p. 524.

Kenneth Drake

"Christ specifically chose the monarchic regime for the Church and designated the person of Saint Peter as the subject of supreme authority" (Fr. Joachim Salaverri).

Church's form of monarchy from that suggested by Saint Thomas as the best form of government for men. The Church's form of monarchy is *pure*, not mixed or tempered, he explains, because the Pope's authority over the Universal Church is total and direct; it is not limited. The only authority above the Pope's is that of God Himself.[25]

Nevertheless, the Church's monarchy is not an *absolute* monarchy, Cardinal Billot explains, since bishops are not mere delegates of the Pope. Bishops enjoy an ordinary and immediate authority over their dioceses, though in submission to the Sovereign Pontiff.[26]

Thus, Cardinal Billot reasons, the Church's form of government is that of a "pure monarchy coupled with an aristocracy."[27] Cardinal Billot calls this a "full and perfect monarchy." His concluding definition reads, "by divine institution, the Church's form of government is that of a *full and perfect monarchy*."[28]

---

25. To say that the authority of the Pope is limited by no other authority on earth does not mean it is discretionary or arbitrary. The Pope, like every man, is subject to moral precepts and especially to the obligations of his office. In other words, as Vicar of Christ, he may not impose his own will on the Church. He can only carry out the will of the One he represents. The will of Christ is clearly manifested in the New Testament, in the writings of the Fathers of the Church, and in the documents issued by the ordinary and extraordinary Magisterium of the Church. It is made even more explicit by Catholic theology.
26. On the direct authority of the Pope over the whole Church, St. Thomas asks how it is possible for a dual jurisdiction, that of the Pope and that of the bishop, to be exerted over the same diocese and the same faithful. He explains that if the two jurisdictions were equal, there would be a conflict and it would not be possible. But this is not the case, since the jurisdictions of the Pope and the bishop are distinct: The first is superior and principal, the second is inferior and subordinate. Both have the same end, and function in harmony (*In IV Sententiarum*, D. 17, Q.3 a.3., q. 5 ad 3um, in Billot, *Tractatus De Ecclesia Christi*, p. 644).
27. "*Monarchia pura aristocratiae coniuncta.*" Billot, *Tractatus De Ecclesia Christi*, p. 531.
28. "*Et ideo regimen Ecclesiae dicendum est divina institutione exactum ad formam plenae perfectaeque monarchiae*," ibid., p. 535. Our emphasis.

THE PRIMACY OF PETER IS THE THEOLOGICAL FOUNDATION FOR PONTIFICAL MONARCHY

This monarchy of the Church has its theological foundation in the Primacy of Saint Peter.

Father Salaverri attests to this: "On the institution of the Church as a monarchy: Christ specifically chose the monarchic regime for the Church and designated the person of Saint Peter as the subject of supreme authority."[29] Father Pesch does likewise: "Christ, by establishing the apostolic college under the primacy of Peter, with authority of jurisdiction and order, founded a religious, hierarchical, and monarchic society that we call His Church."[30]

MODERNISTS DENIED THAT THE EARLY CHURCH WAS A MONARCHY

On December 26, 1910, Saint Pius X, in the Letter "*Ex quo, nono labente*" to the Apostolic Delegates of the Orient, condemned the modernist theory that the early Church did not have a monarchic form of government:

"No less falsely we are asked to believe that in the first centuries the Catholic Church was not the government of one man, that is a monarchy; that the primacy of the Roman Church is not founded on any valid arguments."[31]

THE CHURCH'S "FULL AND PERFECT MONARCHY" WILL LAST UNTIL THE END OF TIME

This "full and perfect monarchy" of the Church cannot change.

29. Salaverri, *De Ecclesia Christi*, in VV.AA, *Sacrae Theologiae Summa*, Vol. I, no. 162.
30. Pesch, *De Ecclesia Christi* in *Compendium Theologiae Dogmaticae*, p. 145.
31. The Monks of Solesmes, *The Church* (Boston: St. Paul Editions, 1980) p. 392.

Cardinal Billot explains in the study mentioned above that the Church's form of government was established by God not in an indirect and *indistinct* manner as was the case in the civil sphere, but in a *direct* and *precise* manner. Thus, it is perfect and permanent. It cannot be modified.[32]

On this unchangeability, Leo XIII teaches:

> Only the Church of Jesus Christ has been able to preserve, and surely will preserve unto the consummation of time, her form of government. Founded by Him Who was, Who is, and Who will be forever (Heb. 13:8), She has received from Him, since Her very origin, all that She requires for the pursuing of Her divine mission across the changeable ocean of human affairs. And, far from wishing to transform Her essential constitution, She has not the power even to relinquish the conditions of true liberty and sovereign independence with which Providence has endowed Her in the general interest of souls."[33]

THE CHURCH IS NOT A DEMOCRACY

The Church never was, is not, and never will be a democracy. Her form of government as instituted by Our Lord is that of a full and perfect monarchy. Were this to change, She would no longer be the Church.

Thus, quoting Cardinal Journet once again, "to call the Church's government 'democratic' is certainly wrong."[34]

32. Billot, *Tractatus De Ecclesia Christi*, p. 526.
33. Leo XIII, Encyclical *Au Milieu de Sollicitudes*, Feb. 16, 1892, n. 17. www.ewtn.com/library/ENCYC/L13CST.HTM
34. Journet, *The Church of the Word Incarnate*, Vol. I, p. 422.

Felipe Barandiaran

The new reformers repeat the old errors of a "democratic" Church promoted by heretics like the Jansenists, followers of Bishop Cornelius Jansen (1585-1638).

Chapter 9

Papal Condemnations of Democracy in the Church

Since the hierarchical structure of the Church is a truth of the Faith, it is not surprising that the Popes uphold this teaching. A sampling of Papal declarations on this point illustrates the importance of this truth.

OLD CONDEMNED HERESIES

In the fourteenth century, Marsilius of Padua, in his book *Defensor Pacis* (*The Defender of Peace*), erroneously maintained that all ecclesiastical power dwells in the Christian people and in the Emperor as their representative. This doctrine was condemned by Pope John XXII as "contrary to the Holy Scriptures, dangerous to the Catholic faith, heretical, and erroneous" and their authors as "undoubtedly heretics and even heresiarchs."[1]

In the seventeenth century, Edmond Richer, in his *De Ecclesiastica et Politica Potestate* (*On Ecclesiastical and Political Power*) espoused the error that the fullness of ecclesiastical power resides in the Church as a whole, which then delegates this power to priests and bishops. Thus, the Pope would be merely the ministerial head of the Church and subject to the college of bishops.[2]

ERRORS OF GALICANISM, JANSENISM, AND FEBRONIANISM

These doctrines were later echoed by Gallicanism[3] and

1. L. Salembier, s.v. "Marsilius of Padua," *Catholic Encyclopedia* (1913), Vol. IX, pp. 720. Cf. Denzinger nos. 495-498.
2. Cf. Pesch, *Compendium Theologiae Dogmaticae*, Vol. 1, no. 276.
3. "A complexus of theories developed in France, especially in the seventeenth

Jansenism[4] and were further spread by Febronianism.

Regarding the last, Friedrich Lauchert writes in the *Catholic Encyclopedia*:

> Febronianism, the politico-ecclesiastical system outlined by Johann Nikolaus von Hontheim, Auxiliary Bishop of Trier, under the pseudonym Justinus Febronius.... He develops...a theory of ecclesiastical organization founded on a denial of the monarchical constitution of the Church. The ostensible purpose was to facilitate the reconciliation of the Protestant bodies with the Church by diminishing the power of the Holy See.[5]

Pope Clement XIII formally condemned these errors. In his turn, Pius VI also condemned them and struggled mightily against Febronianism. He placed Hontheim's work on the *Index of Forbidden Books*, and in his letter "*Post Factum Tibi*" of February 2, 1782, to the Archbishop of Trier, Pius VI reaffirms: "It is, in fact, a dogma of faith that the authority of the bishops, even admitting that it stems directly from Christ, remains dependent on the authority of the Roman Pontiff."[6]

---

century, which tended to restrict the authority of the Church regarding the State (*Political Gallicanism*) or the authority of the Pope regarding councils, bishops, and clergy (*Ecclesiastico-Theological Gallicanism*)." Parente, Piolanti , and Garofalo, *Dictionary of Dogmatic Theology*, p. 108.

4. The theological principles of Cornelius Jansen (1585-1638) emphasize predestination, deny free will, and maintain that human nature is incapable of good. The movement was characterized by general harshness and moral rigor. Its most famous exponent was Pascal. The movement received Papal condemnations (see Denzinger, no. 1291) and its adherents were persecuted in France (though tolerated in the Netherlands) during most of the eighteenth century. From the ecclesiological standpoint, the Jansenists defended democracy in the Church and subordination of the Church to the State (cf. Denzinger, no. 1502).
5. Friedrich Lauchert, s.v. "Febronianism," *Catholic Encyclopedia* (1913), Vol. VI, p. 23.
6. The Monks of Solesmes, *The Church: Papal Teachings* (Boston: St. Paul Editions, 1980), p. 48.

Febronianism became widespread in Germanic countries under the protection of Emperor Joseph II. In 1782, Canon Joseph Valentin Eybel, a prominent leader of the Febronian current, wrote a libel titled *Was ist der Papst*? (*What is the Pope?*). The work rejected papal monarchy and advocated a republican form of government for the Church. In response, Pius VI, in the brief *Super Soliditate* of November 28, 1786, condemned the erroneous proposition "that Christ wished His Church to be governed in the manner of a republic."[7]

These republican theories about the Church are condemned as "containing propositions, respectively false, scandalous, bold, injurious, leading to schism, schismatic, erroneous, leading to heresy, heretical, and some condemned by the Church."[8]

THE CIVIL CONSTITUTION OF THE CLERGY AND THE JANSENIST SYNOD OF PISTOIA

Pius VI also condemned the Civil Constitution of the Clergy. Passed by the National Assembly of Revolutionary France, this decree applied liberal democratic principles to the Church. In the letter *Quod aliquantum* of March 10, 1791, Pius VI condemned the Constitution as schismatic and opposed to the Primacy of Peter.[9]

As the French Revolution reached a climax, Pius VI condemned the errors of the Jansenist Synod of Pistoia in 1794 in the celebrated constitution *Auctorem fidei*. That Synod called for establishment of a democratic system in the Church where power resided in the people—the faithful—who would then designate the Pope, bishops, and parish priests. This Papal document reads:

7. Denzinger, no. 1500.
8. Denzinger, no. 1500, note 1.
9. Cf. The Monks of Solesmes, *The Church: Papal Teachings*, p. 67.

> The proposition which states "that power has been given by God to the Church, that it might be communicated to the pastors who are its ministers for the salvation of souls"; if thus understood that the power of ecclesiastical ministry and of rule is derived from the *community* of the faithful to the pastors,—[is] heretical.[10]

Later, Gallican-Jansenist and liberal elements within the Church tried to prevent the definition of the dogmas of Papal Infallibility and Papal Primacy during the First Vatican Council (1869-1870). Their efforts came to naught. As seen, the dogma of the primacy is the foundation of the monarchic form of government in the Church.[11]

PIUS XII: NO POWER IN THE CHURCH EMANATES FROM THE PEOPLE

Shortly after World War II, Pope Pius XII, in the *Allocution to the Auditors of the Rota* of October 2, 1945, again condemned the opinion that the Church must be transformed into some sort of democracy. Here are a few excerpts from the document.[12] (The subtitles are ours.)

- **Ecclesiastical power differs essentially from civil power**

> If we consider the favorite thesis of democracy (a thesis constantly defended by great Christian thinkers)—that is, that the subject of political power that derives from God is, first and foremost, the peo-

10. Denzinger, no. 1502. Emphasis in original.
11. Chapter 8.
12. *Acta Apost. Sedis*, 1945, pp. 256-62, quoted in Journet, *The Church of the Word Incarnate*, Vol. I, pp. 488-489.

ple (not, indeed, the "masses"), the distinction between Church and State, even a democratic State, becomes ever clearer.... Ecclesiastical power is in fact essentially different from civil power.

- **The origins of the Church, unlike those of civil society, are supernatural**

The origin of the Church, unlike that of the State, does not arise from Natural Law.... The Church derives from a positive act of God which is beyond and above man's social character but in perfect harmony with it.

- **Civil society grows from the bottom upward, while the Church comes to us from above**

This fundamental difference is manifest in one point above all. Unlike the foundation of the State, the foundation of the Church, as a society, was carried out not from below but from above.

- **Christ did not impart His mission as Master, Priest, and Shepherd to the community**

Christ Who, in His Church, has set up the Kingdom of God on earth which He announced and destined for all men and ages, did not hand on to the community of the faithful the mission as Master, Priest, and Shepherd which He received from the Father for the salvation of all men. He handed it on, rather, to a college of Apostles or envoys chosen by Himself so that they should, by their preaching, their priestly ministry, and their social power respectively, bring into the Church the multitude of the faithful in order to sanctify them, enlighten them, and lead them into full maturity as disciples of Christ.

- **The basic subject of power in the Church is never the community of the faithful**

  In the Church, in contradistinction to the State, the basic subject of power and its ultimate manifestation, the supreme judge, is never the community of the faithful. There is thus no popular tribunal or judiciary power emanating from the people in the Church as founded by Christ, and there cannot be.

THE CHURCH IS A HIERARCHICAL SOCIETY

According to Jesuit theologian Fr. Joachim Salaverri, the faithful must believe as a truth of the Faith that the Church is a hierarchical society and not a democracy:

> That the Church, as an institution, is not a democratic society but a hierarchical one was defined by Pius VI against the Synod of Pistoia (Denzinger 1502); against the Protestants by the Council of Trent (Denzinger 960, 966); against the Modernists by Saint Pius X (Denzinger 2145, 3); and against innovators by Vatican Council I (Denzinger 1827s). Therefore, it can be called a defined truth of the faith.[13]

13. Salaverri, *De Ecclesia Christi*, in VV.AA, *Sacrae Theologiae Summa*, Vol. I, no. 130.

Chapter 10

The Principles of Subsidiarity and Authority in the Church

Prof. Leonard Swidler uses the principle of subsidiarity as one of his main arguments for a democratic constitution for the Church.[1] San Francisco's former Archbishop John R. Quinn uses the principle of subsidiarity in his campaign to change the papacy.[2] The democratic changes to the Church's hierarchical structure that Voice of the Faithful proposes are also based on this principle.[3]

There are two errors involved in using the principle of subsidiarity to destroy the Church's hierarchical form of government:

1) a philosophical-sociological error, stemming from a false understanding of the principle of subsidiarity, and
2) a methodological error in drawing theological consequences when applying a philosophical-sociological principle.

We must first analyze the principle of subsidiarity itself, then its false liberal interpretation, and finally the error of applying this interpretation to the Church in detriment to Her theological nature.

---

1. Swidler, *Toward a Catholic Constitution*, p. 149.
2. In his much commented lecture at Oxford on June 29, 1996, he declared: "Large segments of the Catholic Church as well as many Orthodox and other Christians do not believe that collegiality and subsidiarity are being practiced in the Catholic Church in a sufficiently meaningful way." www.usao.edu/~faschaferi/QUINN.HTML. The same idea is found in Archbishop Quinn's book *The Reform of the Papacy* (New York: Herder, 1999), especially Chapters 4–6, pp. 117-177.
3. VOTF Working Paper: *The Problem and Our Vision*.

TFP Archive

Prof. Leonard Swidler is among those who misinterpret the principle of subsidiarity in a liberal egalitarian way. They also err by drawing theological consequences from a philosophical-sociological principle.

THE PRINCIPLE OF SUBSIDIARITY

The principle of subsidiarity is conjoined with the principle of autonomy. The latter consists in a subject's right to provide for his own material, cultural, and spiritual needs without interference from higher authority.

The principle of subsidiarity (from the Latin *subsidium*, subsidy, assistance) can be said to have two aspects: (a) the need for authority to respect a subject's autonomy, and (b) authority's obligation to assist a subject in those areas where the subject's efforts are insufficient.

As Prof. Plinio Corrêa de Oliveira explains:

> The intervention of public authority in the various sectors of the national life must be undertaken in such a way that, as soon as possible, each sector may live with the necessary autonomy. Thus, each family should be allowed to do everything it is capable of doing by its nature, being supported by higher social groups only in a subsidiary way in what is beyond its sphere of action. These groups, in turn, should only receive the help of their municipality in what exceeds their normal capacity, and so on up the line in the relations between the municipality and the region or between the region and the country.[4]

In 1931, Pope Pius XI explicitly referred to the principle of subsidiarity in his encyclical *Quadragesimo Anno*. However, it should be noted that, as a principle of the natural order, subsidiarity was certainly implicit in Leo XIII's social writings.[5] This is how Pius XI formulates this principle in his encyclical:

4. Corrêa de Oliveira, *Revolution and Counter-Revolution*, p. 22.
5. Fr. R. E. Mulcahy, s.v. "Subsidiarity," *New Catholic Encyclopedia* (New York: McGraw Hill, 1967), Vol. XIII, p. 762.

> That most weighty principle, which cannot be set aside or changed, remains fixed and unshaken in social philosophy: Just as it is gravely wrong to take from individuals what they can accomplish by their own initiative and industry and give it to the community, so also it is an injustice and at the same time a grave evil and disturbance of right order to assign to a greater and higher association what lesser and subordinate organizations can do. For every social activity ought of its very nature to furnish help to the members of the body social, and never destroy and absorb them.[6]

John Paul II also discusses the principle of subsidiarity, saying:

> A community of a higher order should not interfere in the internal life of a community of a lower order, depriving the latter of its functions, but rather should support it in case of need and help to coordinate its activity with the activities of the rest of society, always with a view to the common good.[7]

In his *Christian Social Doctrine*, Joseph Cardinal Höffner explains when—according to the principle of subsidiarity—the intervention of higher authority is necessary:

> On the other hand, subsidiarity means "help from above," which at times is tendentiously overlooked. This helping intervention of the larger social units can be necessary for two reasons: first, because individual people or smaller social circles can fail culpably or

6. Pius XI, Encyclical *Quadragesimo Anno*, May 15, 1931 (Washington, D.C.: National Catholic Welfare Conference, 1942), no. 79, p. 30.
7. John Paul II, Encyclical *Centesimus Annus*, May 15, 1991, no. 48. www.ewtn/library/ENCYC/ JP2HUNDR.HTM. Cf. *Catechism of the Catholic Church*, no. 1883.

> inculpably in the field of duties proper to them; second, because it is a question of tasks that can only be mastered by the more comprehensive social units.[8]

In *Quadragesimo Anno*, Pius XI fought the totalitarian and centralizing tendency of modern times, especially socialism and the techno-bureaucracy that drowns the individual and smaller communities in a tidal wave of laws, regulations, and federal or state planning.

FALSE LIBERAL NOTION OF THE PRINCIPLE OF SUBSIDIARITY

The principle of subsidiarity, however, has often been misunderstood. As Fr. R. E. Mulcahy, S.J., observes, many people, imbued with the nineteenth century's spirit of liberalism, want to give the principle of subsidiarity a quasi-anarchical interpretation. In so doing, these liberals hurl subsidiarity at authority in an effort to abolish the latter. They see authority, at best, as a necessary or tolerated evil.

Father Mulcahy points out that John XXIII deals with this erroneous interpretation in his encyclical *Mater et Magistra*. Recognizing authority's right to intervene, the Pope shows how the principles of subsidiarity and authority must work together, with the higher authority able to intervene whenever necessary. In the words of the encyclical: "In this work of directing, stimulating, co-ordinating, supplying, and integrating, its [the civil power's] guiding principle must be the 'principle of subsidiary function' formulated by Pius XI in *Quadragesimo Anno*."[9]

8. Joseph Cardinal Höffner, *Christian Social Teaching*, trans. by Stephen Wentworth-Arndt and Gerald Finan (Bratislava: Lúc, 1997), p. 52.
9. John XXIII, Encyclical *Mater et Magistra* (May 15, 1961), in *The Encyclicals and Other Messages of John XXIII* (Washington, D.C.: TPS Press, 1964), p. 263.

BASIC PRINCIPLES OF A WHOLESOME SOCIAL ORDER

Scholars of political philosophy and Catholic Social Doctrine specify three basic principles in a wholesome social order: authority, solidarity, and subsidiarity.[10]

These three principles must work together for the common good. While all three are necessary, the principle of authority provides the *unity* and *finality* of society.

As is readily seen, an imbalance in any of these three principles can harm the common good. An exaggeration of solidarity leads to collectivism; an exaggeration of subsidiarity leads to anarchy; and an excess of authority leads to tyranny, as is evident with totalitarian regimes.

Cardinal Höffner distinguishes the principle of subsidiarity from that of solidarity:

> The principle of subsidiarity presupposes the principles of solidarity and the common good, but is not identical with them. That society must help the individual is a clear statement of the solidarity principle, which emphasizes mutual connection and obligation; the distribution and delimitation of the competence to be considered in this help fall to the subsidiarity principle.[11]

Thus, authority's proper use of the principle of subsidiarity regulates the principle of solidarity. The principle of subsidiarity, however, is not the *directing* or *leading* principle of society.

10. Their terminology, however, is not uniform. Heinrich Rommen, for example, writes: "Social life is governed by the principles of autonomy, of hierarchy and intervention" (Heinrich A. Rommen, *The State in Catholic Thought* [St. Louis: Herder, 1945], p. 302).
11. Höffner, *Christian Social Teaching*, p. 51.

THE PRINCIPLE OF AUTHORITY

The directive role in a wholesome social order belongs to the principle of authority. Society's good functioning requires that the purpose for which it exists be assured by the firm action of government.

Fr. Baltasar Pérez Argos explains the irreplaceable role of the principle of authority in a wholesome social order:

> If solidarity and subsidiarity are the fundamental principles of the organization of the social order that on the one hand give man the support he needs to live a truly human life (GS, 26) and, on the other, do so without prejudice to his freedom, we must also add another principle: that of authority. Without the principle of authority, social order would have neither the solidity nor the efficacy necessary to accomplish what is expected of it, which we call the *common good*. The principle of authority is complementary to the other two. This principle affirms the need for the existence, in every well-organized society, of a moral force capable of efficaciously guiding the action of all of the members that compose it toward achieving the common good of that society.[12]

In exercising the principle of authority, government must always show due respect for legitimate autonomies and limit its intervention to maintaining order and otherwise furthering society's general goals.[13]

12. Fr. Baltasar Pérez Argos, S.J., "Los Cuatro Pilares de la Doctrina Social," in *Verbo*, March-April 1991, p. 333.
13. Ibid., pp. 332-333.

IMPORTANCE OF AUTHORITY IN THE CHURCH

The principle of authority in the Church, as a society of the faithful,[14] is even more important than in temporal society. This importance stems from the fact that the act of faith is based on the authority of God revealing and on the authority of the Church teaching what must be believed.[15]

This is why Father Lercher states that "one may say that authority is the *formal cause* of the Church as a visible society."[16]

Civil society, which belongs to the natural order, and ecclesiastical society (the Church), which belongs to the supernatural order,[17] are analogous but not identical.[18]

Government in civil society has a purely natural origin and is derived from historical circumstances. On the contrary, the Church's hierarchy has a supernatural origin and was divinely instituted. Thus, the Church's hierarchical structure is unique, essentially different from government in civil society.

Another difference is that the exercise of authority in civil society does not imprint an indelible character on its holder. While dynasties end up acquiring a sacred character, as it were, this takes place only in the natural and symbolic order. It is different in the Church. Even if a person is assigned to a post by human means, he enters the Sacred Hierarchy only when he

14. Saint Robert Bellarmine's classic definition of the Church: "A body of men *united together by the profession of the same Christian Faith*, and by participation in the same sacraments, *under the governance of lawful pastors*, more especially of the Roman Pontiff, the sole vicar of Christ on earth." Quoted in G. H. Joyce, *s.v.* "Church," in *Catholic Encyclopedia*, Vol. III, p. 745. Our emphasis.
15. Cf. Leo XIII, Encyclical *Satis Cogitum*, June 29, 1896, no. 9. www.ewtn/library/ENCYC/L13SATIS.HTM
16. Lercher, *Institutiones Theologiae Dogmaticae*, p. 240.
17. Pius XI: "Now, necessary societies are three in number...; of these, two, namely, the family and civil society, are of the natural order; and the third, the Church, to be sure, is of the supernatural order" Denzinger, 2203. Cf. Salaverri, *De Ecclesia Christi*, in VV.AA, *Sacrae Theologiae Summa*, Vol. I, no. 927.
18. Cf. Salaverri, *De Ecclesia Christi*, in VV.AA, *Sacrae Theologiae Summa*, Vol. I, p. 827.

receives the sacramental character of the plenitude of Holy Orders.[19]

Therefore, Church government, as an institution, differs in nature from civil government, since She is divinely instituted and has a sacramental basis, founded on the sacrament of Holy Orders. This difference must always be kept in mind when applying the principle of authority to the Church.

RIGHT APPLICATION OF THE PRINCIPLE OF SUBSIDIARITY WITHIN THE CHURCH

When applying the principle of subsidiarity, reformists often quote Pius XII's words that it is valid "also for the life of the Church." They omit, however, his important qualifier: "with due regard for her hierarchical structure."[20]

Thus, the principle of subsidiarity applies to the Church provided it is in harmony with and subordinate to the Church's theological nature, that is, respectful of the authority of the Pope and bishops to teach, govern, and sanctify the faithful. Thus, the principle of subsidiarity must be adjusted to accommodate the Church's supernatural and natural realities.

While Christ entrusted the hierarchy with the mission to teach, govern, and sanctify the faithful, the latter, by Baptism and Confirmation, have the right to provide for their own spiritual necessities without undue interference from ecclesiastical authority. Furthermore, the faithful have the right, and at times the duty, to help the spiritual common good of both temporal society and the Church Herself, for they are members of both.

There are certain spiritual necessities, on the other hand, that the faithful cannot provide for themselves. For example, they depend on priestly ministry for sacramental life.

19. Cf. Gréa, *De L'Église*, p. 100.
20. Pius XII, "La elevateza," in *Discorsi e Radiomessaggi di Sua Santità Pio XII*, p. 389.

As in temporal society, the exercise of individual autonomy in the Church cannot be exercised in detriment to the spiritual common good or the disturbance of ecclesiastical public order.

THE RIGHT OF ASSOCIATION IN THE CHURCH

The right of association in the Church is a clear example of the proper application of the principle of subsidiarity to the Church.

Any member of the faithful has the right to undertake initiatives that further the apostolate, charity, piety, the spreading of sound doctrine, a more perfect life, or imbuing society with the spirit of the Gospel.[21] The exercise of this right is not subject to ecclesiastical intervention. Like anything else, nevertheless, it is subject to ecclesiastical vigilance in matters of faith and morals.

This notwithstanding, Canon Law reserves exclusively to ecclesiastical authority the establishment of associations that spread Catholic doctrine *in the name of the Church* as well as those that promote public worship or other activities whose nature is reserved to the ecclesiastical authority.[22]

This is understandable, since public worship is that which is rendered in the name of the Church by persons duly appointed for this purpose and according to formulations established by competent ecclesiastical authority. By the same token, the spreading of Catholic doctrine in the name of the Church involves the hierarchy's responsibility, and so requires the hierarchy's control.

Canon Law also foresees the hypothesis of ecclesiastical authority exercising the principle of subsidiarity even in a field not restricted by nature and normally left to the private initiative of the faithful. The hierarchy can intervene and establish

21. See Canons 215, 225 § 1, 298 § 1.
22. Canon 301 § 1.

its own associations when the private initiative of the faithful is not up to the task: "Competent ecclesiastical authority, if it judges it expedient, can also erect associations of Christian faithful in order to attain directly or indirectly other spiritual ends whose accomplishment has not been sufficiently provided for by the efforts of private persons."[23]

In all the above, we see a balanced application of the principle of subsidiarity, with no violation of the Church's hierarchical structure by the faithful, and no violation of the faithful's autonomy by ecclesiastical authority.

FAITHFUL MEMBERS OF THE MYSTICAL BODY OF CHRIST

There is nothing totalitarian or dictatorial about the Church. Inspired as She is by the Holy Spirit, sanctity and apostolic zeal do not depend on one's personal position within the Church but on fidelity to grace.

As seen, the faithful do not hold a merely passive position in the Church. They are members of the Mystical Body of Christ and, as such, must do everything to propagate Christ's doctrines and morals in the world in the manner of true apostles. They must be concerned about the Church and zealous for Her. However, they must at the same time "hold the traditions" they "have learned"[24] from the perennial Magisterium of the Church.

The Church has always respected and fostered the true liberty of the children of God. There is nothing truly good that is off-limits in the Church, be it for the faithful or the clergy, provided the nature of the Church and Her sacramental character and powers of jurisdiction are respected.

This enormous liberty explains why Church history is so

23. Canon 301 § 2.
24. 2 Thess. 2:14.

rich with apostolic initiatives and new forms of religious or associative life.

Hence, there is the vigor and strength of Catholic laity in a Saint Louis IX of France, who was a model Christian ruler and warrior. There were such journalists as a Louis Veuillot, who devoted his writings to defending Catholic truth. There is a Prof. Plinio Corrêa de Oliveira, whose thought and action attracted so many young men to dedicate their lives to the Church and the restoration of Christian civilization.

There is the marvelous proliferation of religious orders, the blossoming of congregations, the countless number of charitable, educational, and apostolic lay associations, the fruitful action of lay people in politics, arts, science, and all fields of human activity.

There is today the great freedom with which the laity form associations and movements to educate the public on the evils of abortion, to promote home schooling, parental rights, the traditional Latin liturgy, Perpetual Adoration, the Rosary, and so much more. No member of the faithful is forbidden to practice or promote a legitimate devotion.[25]

It is one thing, however, for the faithful to have full liberty to act in their proper sphere. It is something altogether different to usurp the rights of the Hierarchy in the name of freedom, while complaining that there is not enough freedom to successfully carry out that usurpation.

25. See. John Paul II, Apostolic Exhortation *Christi Fideles Laici*, on the Vocation and the Mission of the Lay Faithful in the Church and in the World, Dec. 30, 1988, www.ewtn/library/PAPALDOC/JP2LAICI.HTM. See also Canons 204-231.

CHAPTER 11

The Apostolic Origins of Clerical Celibacy and Church Tradition

CELIBACY: CAUSE OF PSYCHOLOGICAL AND SPIRITUAL DAMAGE?

In the wake of the sexual scandals, many are the voices demanding the abolition of clerical celibacy.

Voice of the Faithful says it does not take a position in this matter, but included several married priests among the speakers at its July 2002 Boston convention. These criticized priestly celibacy either openly or indirectly.[1]

One of them, the former priest Anthony T. Massimini, in an essay referred to as "The Guide" by VOTF leadership[2] and recommended as must reading for everyone planning on attending the convention, called for the abolition of priestly celibacy. He acknowledged that there is no direct link between celibacy and pedophilia, but affirmed that only a tiny number of priests have the gift of celibacy and claimed that because Church teaching insists on priestly celibacy, "the psychological and spiritual damage being done to the Church is immense."[3] Mr. Massimini based his convention address on this essay.

PRIESTLY CELIBACY AND THE INDISSOLUBILITY OF MARRIAGE

Self-appointed reformers always emerge in times of crises, offering "brilliant" solutions that attempt to demolish the

1. See Chapter 3.
2. VOTF, *Weekly Voice*, July 5, 2002.
3. Anthony T. Massimini, "Discerning the Spirit: A Guide for Renewing and Restructuring the Catholic Church," www.votf.org/Educating_ Ourselves/massimini.html.

Church's most venerable traditions. Priestly celibacy, a glorious trait of the Latin Church, has been a constant target of these so-called reformers.

Curiously enough, calls for the abolition of priestly celibacy go hand-in-hand with efforts to destroy the indissolubility of marriage. This is easily understood since both positions are based on the idea that chastity is impossible to observe. Historically, this happened with Eastern Orthodox schismatics, Protestants, Anglicans, and others. The total or partial abolition of priestly celibacy either accompanied or followed acceptance of divorce.

FALSE ARGUMENTS AGAINST CELIBACY

In addition to pseudo-scientific arguments used to prove the impossibility of observing chastity, there are frequent claims that celibacy is a purely disciplinary policy dating not from Apostolic times but introduced into Church legislation only at a later date. Having been so introduced, it can be abolished or at least made optional.

Many studies, some quite recent, debunk this pseudo historic-canonical argument. Among the most important of these are *Apostolic Origins of Priestly Celibacy* by Fr. Christian Cochini, S.J., *The Case for Clerical Celibacy* by Alfons Maria Cardinal Stickler, and *Celibacy in the Early Church* by Fr. Stefan Heid.[4]

EARLY CHURCH TRADITION

With solid documentation, these authors show that while

4. Fr. Christian Cochini, S.J. *Apostolic Origins of Priestly Celibacy* (San Francisco: Ignatius Press, 1990); Alfons Maria Cardinal Stickler, *The Case for Clerical Celibacy* (San Francisco: Ignatius Press, 1995); Fr. Stefan Heid, *Celibacy in the Early Church* (San Francisco: Ignatius Press, 2000).

one cannot speak of celibacy in the strict sense of the word (never having been married), it is certain that since Apostolic times the Church has had as a norm that men elevated to the diaconate, priesthood, and episcopate were required to observe continence.

Cardinal Stickler—a well-regarded Canon Law historian, an expert on Roman Congregations, and former head of the Vatican Library—explains that both Apostolic and early Church practice did not require a man to be single or widowed in order to be ordained.

A large number of Christians were adult converts (a typical example is Saint Augustine, who converted when he was 30), making it common for married men to be ordained as priests or designated as bishops. Nevertheless, married candidates were expected to discontinue all marital relations and even cease dwelling under the same roof with their spouses. If a spouse refused her full and free consent to either measure, the candidate was not ordained. Often, the consenting spouse herself made a commitment to retire to a community of women religious where she lived in perfect chastity.

In their case for married priests, reformists cite words of Saint Paul in his Epistles to Titus and Timothy that a bishop had to be a "man of only one woman."[5] Cardinal Stickler explains, however, that according to the interpretation commonly adopted in the early Church (and attested to by the Fathers of the Church), this teaching of Saint Paul meant that a candidate could not have been married twice. In other words, remarried widowers were ineligible for the office of bishop. Early Church officials doubted that a remarried widower would have the strength to fulfill the two requirements, that is, the discontinuance of both marital relations and joint dwelling with the second spouse under the same roof.

5. 1 Tim. 3:2; 3:12; Titus 1:6.

THE APOSTOLIC TRADITION

The only Apostle known to have been married is Saint Peter, whose mother-in-law is mentioned in the Gospels. While other Apostles may have been married, it is nevertheless clear that all of them left everything, including their families, to follow Christ. One reads in the Gospels that Saint Peter said to Our Lord, "We left all things, and have followed Thee." The Divine Master answered: "Amen, I say to you, there is no man that hath left house, or parents, or brethren, or wife, or children for the kingdom of God's sake, who shall not receive much more in this present time and, in the world to come life everlasting."[6]

EARLY CHURCH COUNCILS REAFFIRM PRIESTLY CELIBACY

This brief overview does not cover the whole history of celibacy so amply documented by Cardinal Stickler. Space permits only some of the most outstanding cases.

The Council of Elvira in Spain (310) dealt with priestly chastity (Canon 33), and presented perfect continence as a norm that must be maintained and observed, and not as an innovation. The lack of any revolt or surprise attests to its already widespread practice.

At the Council of the Church of Africa (390) and, above all, at the Council of Carthage (419), which Saint Augustine attended, similar norms were adopted. These councils recalled the ecclesiastical praxis of the obligation of perfect chastity, affirming that such praxis is of Apostolic tradition.

Pope Siricius, answering a specific consultation about clerical celibacy in 385, affirmed that bishops and priests who continue marital relations after ordination violate an irrevocable

6. Luke 18:28-30. Cf. Matt. 19:27-30, and Mark 10:20-21.

TFP Archive

Alfons Maria Cardinal Stickler's book *The Case for Clerical Celibacy* proves the Apostolic tradition of priestly celibacy.

TFP Archive

Married former-priest Anthony Massimini attacked priestly celibacy at the VOTF convention as the cause of immense psychological and spiritual damage.

law dating from the very inception of the Church binding them to continence.

Several other Popes and regional councils, particularly in Gaul (present-day France) continued to recall the tradition of celibacy and to punish abuses.

Saint Gregory VII, when struggling against the intervention of the Holy Roman Emperor in ecclesiastical affairs, had to fight simony, the purchase of Church posts, and Nicolaitism, a heresy that advocated, among other things, priestly marriage. Because of this struggle, some mistakenly conclude that Saint Gregory VII introduced the law of celibacy into the Church. Saint Gregory VII, and later the Second Lateran Council (1139), did not introduce the law but simply confirmed that it was in force and issued regulations for its observance. Since by then most recruiting for the priesthood was done among the unmarried, the Council forbade priestly marriage, declaring it to be null and void in the case of priests, deacons, or anyone with a solemn vow of religion.

THE CASE OF PAPHNUTIUS

The main argument of those who deny the Apostolic tradition of priestly continence comes from an incident linked to the first Council of Nicea (325). Paphnutius, an Egyptian bishop, was reported to have protested in the name of tradition when the Council Fathers sought to impose priestly continence. Because of his protest, the Council is said to have refused to impose such continence.

Cardinal Stickler ably refutes this claim. He points out that Eusebius of Cesarea, who was present during the whole event and was the Council's historian, makes no reference to any such protest, which he certainly would have noted had it really happened.

The story of Paphnutius first appears almost a century later in the writings of two Byzantine authors, Socrates and Sozomen. The first cites as his source his conversation as a young man with an elderly man who claimed to have been at the Council of Nicea. The veracity of this story is questionable since Socrates was born more than fifty years after the Council. His interlocutor would have had to be at least seventy years old when he was born and practically in his nineties at the time of the supposed conversation.

Further, this story of a supposed protest was always looked upon with disbelief because Paphnutius's name is not on the roster of Council Fathers who came from Egypt. This fact is stated by Valesius, the editor of Socrates and Sozomen's works, in Migne's *Greek Patrology*.

Still, for Cardinal Stickler the decisive argument against the Paphnutius story comes from the Second Council of Trullo (691). During this Council of the Eastern Church, the Council Fathers, under pressure from the Byzantine Emperor, allowed marriage for priests (but not for bishops), breaking with tradition in both East and West. These Council Fathers, who needed to justify their rupture with the tradition of priestly continence, failed to present the supposed testimony of Paphnutius, which would have bolstered their case. Instead, they invoked the Council of Carthage, which, as seen above, does not support their position. To make their case, these Council Fathers resorted to misrepresenting the Council of Carthage's decrees, a fact even schismatic historians now acknowledge. The Western Church never accepted this rupture with tradition by the Second Council of Trullo.

Cardinal Stickler laments that such well-known historians as Funk, at the end of the nineteenth century, accepted the story of Paphnutius at face value, even though many of his contemporaries had already rejected it. Among others responsible for spreading this error was E. Vacandard in the prestigious *Dictionnaire de Théologie Catholique*.

PARTICIPATION IN THE PRIESTHOOD OF OUR LORD

Finally, Cardinal Stickler argues that the reason for priestly celibacy is not a functional one. Unlike the Old Testament, where the priesthood was merely a temporary function received by way of inheritance, the priesthood in the New Testament is a vocation, a calling that transforms the person and confiscates him entirely. In the New Testament, the priest is a sanctifier, a mediator.

Priesthood in the New Testament is a participation in the Priesthood of Our Lord Jesus Christ, the High Priest. The priest has a mysterious and special bond with Christ, in Whose name and by Whose power he offers the bloodless sacrifice (*in persona Christi*). The most profound reason for priestly celibacy comes from this supernatural bond with the Savior.

THE APOSTOLIC EXHORTATION "*PASTORES DABO VOBIS*"

In the March 25, 1992, post-synodal Apostolic Exhortation *Pastores Dabo Vobis* (On the Formation of Priests Today) addressed to all bishops, Pope John Paul II recalled the spiritual reasons for priestly celibacy and its present timeliness. He says:

> Referring to the evangelical counsels, the Council states that "preeminent among these counsels is that precious gift of divine grace given to some by the Father (cf. Matt. 19:11; 1 Cor. 7:7) in order more easily to devote themselves to God alone with an undivided heart (cf. 1 Cor. 7:32-34) in virginity or celibacy. This perfect continence for love of the kingdom of heaven has always been held in high esteem by the

> Church as a sign and stimulus of love, and as a singular source of spiritual fertility in the world."...
>
> It is especially important that the priest understand the theological motivation of the Church's law on celibacy. Inasmuch as it is a law, it expresses the Church's will, even before the will of the subject expressed by his readiness. But the will of the Church finds its ultimate motivation in the link between celibacy and sacred ordination, which configures the priest to Jesus Christ the Head and Spouse of the Church. The Church, as the Spouse of Jesus Christ, wishes to be loved by the priest in the total and exclusive manner in which Jesus Christ, Her Head and Spouse, loved her. Priestly celibacy, then, is the gift of self in and with Christ to his Church and expresses the priest's service to the Church in and with the Lord.[7]

AN IDENTITY CRISIS

As Cardinal Stickler points out, the main reason celibacy is questioned today is because the clergy faces an identity crisis. Only by restoring the true identity of the priest can the profound reasons for celibacy be understood and practiced. This crisis is not resolved by "returning to the origins of the Church," a solution proposed by proponents of married priests and their sympathizers. Those origins simply do not allow a priest to cohabit with his wife and continue exercising his priestly ministry.

7. John Paul II, Apostolic Exhortation *Pastores Dabo Vobis*, (March 25, 1992), www.vatican.va/holy_father/john_paul_ii/apost_exhortations/documents/hf_jp-ii_exh_25031992_pastores-dabo-vobis_en.html.

Christ chose His Apostles from among men and it has been "consistently held that the exclusion of women from the priesthood is in accordance with God's plan for his Church." (Letter *Ordinatio Sacerdotalis*).

CHAPTER 12

The Priestly Ordination of Women: a Theological Impossibility

The push for a "democratic" Church and the agitation for women priests both stem from the same radical egalitarianism. For this very reason, they often go hand in hand. Thus it is only appropriate to recall some of the main lines of Church teaching on the theological impossibility of women priests.[1]

VOTF'S PRETENDED SILENCE ON WOMEN PRIESTS

VOTF's official neutrality on women priests appears to be tactical, not ideological. Dr. James Muller, its founder, explains:

> We've got to stay focused. Our goal is to organize the laity and give us a voice. If we start fighting over the gay issue, married priests and everything else, we won't make it.[2]
>
> We are not getting into issues of women priests or papal infallibility. These are not our issues.[3]

These statements notwithstanding, several speakers at VOTF's Boston convention in July 2002 are linked with the women's ordination movement,[4] and Fr. William Kremmell

1. Cf. Francisco A. P. Sola, S.J., *De sacramentis vitae socialis christianae seu De sacramentis ordinis et matrimonii,* in *Sacrae Theologiae Summa*, (Madrid: Biblioteca de Autores Cristianos, 1956), Vol. IV, p. 597-698. H. Noldin, S.J., A. Schmitt, S. J., G. Heinzel, S.J. *Summa Theologiae Moralis* (Innsbruck: Feliciani Rauch, 1962), Vol. III, p. 387-425.
2. Mary Rourke, "Staking Their Claim," *The Los Angeles Times*.
3. Miriam Hill, "Catholic Group in Boston Sows Seeds of Revolution," *The Philadelphia Inquirer*, (May 15, 2002).
4. See Chapter 3.

"opened the Mass by noting that 25 years ago any Catholic convention of this size would have tried to persuade a bishop to celebrate Mass for them.... In 25 years, 'hopefully,' a married woman might be presiding over such a Mass."[5]

Furthermore, in the VOTF paper, "The Guide," married priest Anthony Massimini echoes numerous women ordination leaders: "Early Christian leaders went so far as to erroneously regard Mary Magdalene, a close friend of Jesus and a highly respected Christian woman, who was a leader in the early church, as a prostitute. The clerical culture picked up this negative mindset."[6]

RADICAL EGALITARIANISM, A COMMON DENOMINATOR BETWEEN A "DEMOCRATIC" CHURCH AND WOMEN PRIESTS

The statements of Sr. Christine Schenk, director of Future Church, show the radical egalitarianism common to both a "democratic" Church and the push for women priests:

> I think what this crisis points to is, we need to take back the church.... Catholic Church leadership rests solely in the hands of celibate men. What I think has happened historically is a massive "not-dealing" with sexuality in a healthy way.... So women, and anything having to do with women are verboten; women, and men married to women, can't be ordained.[7]

---

5. Paulson, "Lay Catholics Issue Call to Transform Their Church," *The Boston Globe*, July 21, 2002.
6. Cf. Anthony T. Massimini, "Discerning the Spirit," www.votf.org/Educating_Ourselves/massimini.html.
7. Quoted in Suzanne Batchelor "Catholic Women Call for Radical Change Within," *Women's Enews*, April 21, 2002, www.womensenews.org/article.cfm/dyn/aid/885/context/cover/.

Another nun making the connection is Sr. Maureen Fiedler, S.L., the U.S. representative of We Are Church. She spoke at a Detroit Call to Action conference in November 1996 on We Are Church's signature drive pressuring the Vatican for reform:

> Regarding the referendum's call for women priests, Sister Fiedler said, "priesthood includes the office of bishop." Someone from the audience yelled out, "Pope too." Sister Fiedler replied: "Right, Pope too. I dare say some of us would probably assume the office long enough to abolish it. Or at least transform it significantly into something that really looks like a democratic mode of operation."[8]

The radical egalitarianism underlying the movement for women's ordination clashes head-on with Church doctrine and tradition.

GOD DECIDES THE KIND OF WORSHIP AND MINISTER PLEASING TO HIM

According to Natural Law, men must recognize their dependence in relation to God by rendering Him the supreme cult of *latria* (adoration). This worship, both in public and in private, has been rendered to Him from the beginning of mankind.

As a general rule, in early times the heads of families, elders, or community leaders were picked to lead the public worship. With the growth of humanity, a class with specific priestly functions was established. Thus, in the Old Testament, God designated the tribe of Levi from among the Jews as the tribe from which priests were chosen.[9]

8. David Finnigan, "'We Are Church' Signature Drive Shows Few Gains," *National Catholic Register*, Dec. 8-14, 1996.
9. Cf. Exod. 28:1; Num. 3:5-6.

God, the Supreme Lord and Creator, has the right to decide what type of worship and minister is pleasing to Him. Consequently, the only acceptable type of worship or priesthood is that which He Himself established.

GOD CHOSE ONLY MEN FOR THE PRIESTHOOD

Even in the Old Testament, God picked only men for the priestly ministry. Thus, in accordance with Mosaic Law, the priesthood was entrusted exclusively to Aaron,[10] from the tribe of Levi, and to his male offspring.[11]

Likewise, in the New Testament, making use of His supreme liberty and authority, the Word Incarnate again chose only men to be priests. Thus, women were excluded from this priesthood by Divine will.

The main argument of those advocating women priests is that Jesus made this choice merely as a concession to the prevailing culture. To claim that He was moved by cultural, sociological, or any other human reason is to doubt His infinite wisdom, prudence, and judgment. This is tantamount to denying His Divinity.

Another argument is that the Church has power over the Sacraments and can change what would amount to no more than a disciplinary measure, thus admitting women to Holy Orders. The answer is that the Church has power over the sacraments only in their accidents, not over what was instituted by Christ Himself, such as bread and wine for the Eucharist, water for Baptism, and so forth. This also applies to the priesthood wherein the manifest will of Christ—which is therefore a positive Divine commandment—was that only men be called to the priestly ministry.[12]

10. Cf. Num. 3:10; 16:1ff; 17:5; 18:7.
11. Cf. Exod. 28ff.; Lev. 6; Num. 16:17. Also, A. Stöger, "Sacerdocio," in Johannes B. Bauer, *Diccionario de Teología Bíblica* (Barcelona: Herder, 1967), cols. 946-958.
12. Cf. Congregation for Doctrine of Faith, *Inter Insigniores—Declaration on the*

"LET WOMEN KEEP SILENCE IN THE CHURCHES"

Saint Paul teaches:

> Let women keep silence in the churches: for it is not permitted them to speak, but to be subject, as also the Law says. But if they would learn any thing, let them ask their husbands at home. For it is a shame for a woman to speak in the church.[13]
>
> Let the woman learn in silence, with all subjection. But I suffer not a woman to teach, nor to use authority over man: but to be in silence.[14]

Now if women must neither teach nor speak in church or have authority over men, with much greater reason they are not permitted to offer the sacrifice, a function which from history's earliest days presumed command and preeminence, as seen above.[15]

This was the position of Christ Himself, the practice of the Apostles, and the constant tradition of the Church.

THE CATHOLIC PRIEST PARTICIPATES IN THE ETERNAL PRIESTHOOD OF CHRIST

Christ is the true Priest, established by God from all eterni-

Admission of Women to the Ministerial Priesthood, www.ewtn.com/library/CURIA/CDFINSIG.HTM.

13. 1 Cor. 14:34-35.
14. 1 Tim. 2:11-12.
15. Feminists argue for reform based on recent cultural changes in women's behavior. But the Church does not base Her doctrine on the ebb and flow of social or cultural changes, but on the sources of Revelation, that is, Scripture and Tradition. Moreover, the authoritative interpreter of Revelation is the Magisterium of the Church, not theologians or the faithful, let alone sociologists and anthropologists.

ty,[16] Who offered "a perfect sacrifice" to God the Father on the altar of the Cross. The specific function of the priest is to offer sacrifice. Now then, the only sacrifice accepted by God in the New Testament is the sacrifice of Christ. Therefore, only Christ's priesthood is now accepted by God. Christ's priesthood abolished all others.

Since Christ is a priest forever[17] and since He is no longer visibly present on earth, His priesthood would not be visible unless men were able to participate in it.

Since Christ founded the Church as a visible society, visible priests have to exist to offer the sacrifice in Her name. Thus, in Christ's Law, the New Testament, there is a twofold priesthood: one that is invisible and another that is visible.

The invisible priesthood is that exercised by Christ, Who is the main priest offering the Sacrifice of the Mass. The visible priesthood is entrusted to men who assume the role of Christ at Mass. This is called the *ministerial* priesthood.

In addition to this ministerial priesthood, which participates in the priesthood of Christ through the sacrament of Holy Orders, there is the *spiritual* or *common* priesthood of the faithful. The latter results from the moral union of all faithful with Christ, the Head of the Mystical Body. Through this spiritual priesthood, the faithful, united with Christ through Baptism, offer the internal sacrifice of their good actions that render glory to God.

In September 2002, John Paul II reminded everyone of this truth while addressing a group of Brazilian bishops in their *ad limina* visit:

> Through Baptism, all of the faithful participate in Christ's priesthood. This is what we call the "common

16. Cf. Heb. 5:6; Ps. 110:5
17. Heb. 7:24.

> priesthood of the faithful." Besides this priesthood, and to serve it, there exists another participation in Christ's mission, that of the ministry conferred by the Sacrament of Holy Orders (*Catechism of the Catholic Church*, 1591), in other words the "ministerial priesthood."

The Pontiff further emphasized that these two priesthoods, the common and the ministerial, differ from one another "not only in degree," but "in essence."[18]

When He instituted the Holy Sacrifice of the Mass and the Sacrament of the Holy Eucharist during the Last Supper, Christ commanded the Apostles, "Do this for a commemoration of Me."[19] Through these words, together with the precept, Christ communicated to the Apostles the power to fulfill it. In other words, He conferred on them priestly power, the power to offer the bloodless sacrifice of the altar.

The Sacrament of Holy Orders is centered on the Holy Eucharist. The Holy Eucharist itself is a sacrament intended for distribution to the faithful. The latter, however, must fulfill the required conditions to receive this great Sacrament, the first of which is to be in the state of grace. Thus, it was appropriate that those who have the power to consecrate bread and wine into the Body and Blood of Christ also have the power to prepare the faithful to receive the Sacrament by conferring upon them or restoring them to the state of grace. Accordingly, the Apostles received the power to baptize and to absolve sins.

The powers of absolution, teaching, ministering to, and governing were bestowed on the Apostles by Our Lord Jesus Christ after the Resurrection.[20]

---

18. Address of Pope John Paul II to the Bishops of Brazil's Regions West 1 and 2 in their *ad limina apostolorum* visit, September 21, 2002 (Our translation from the Portuguese).
19. Luke 22:19; 1 Cor. 11:24.
20. John 20:21-23; Matt. 28:19-20.

THE PRIEST TAKES THE PLACE OF CHRIST

According to the common teaching of theologians, as the priest pronounces the words of Consecration ("This is My Body...") and sacramental absolution ("I absolve you from your sins"), he lends his being, as it were, to Christ. That is why it is said that the priest takes the place of Christ, acting *in persona Christi.*

This point is very well summarized by Fr. Kenneth Baker:

> The priest takes the place of Christ and Christ was a man, not a woman. The sacraments use natural signs to signify spiritual realities. Holy Orders is a sacrament—therefore it is a sign. When the priest says, "This is My Body..." or "I absolve you from your sins," he is taking the place of Christ. Only a man can do that. If a woman tried to act as a priest, the sign value of the sacrament would be lost.[21]

"IT IS NOT ADMISSIBLE TO ORDAIN WOMEN TO THE PRIESTHOOD."

This is the constant teaching of the Church[22] and was recalled by John Paul II in his Apostolic Letter *Ordinatio Sacerdotalis* of May 22, 1994:

> Priestly ordination, which hands on the office entrusted by Christ to his Apostles of teaching, sanctifying, and governing the faithful, has in the Catholic Church from the beginning always been reserved to

21. Fr. Kenneth Baker, S.J., *Fundamentals of Catholicism* (San Francisco: Ignatius Press, 1985), Vol. III, p. 332.
22. Only a few heretics of the early times such as the Pepucians, Marcionites, and Coliridians denied this teaching.

men alone. This tradition has also been faithfully maintained by the Oriental Churches.

When the question of the ordination of women arose in the Anglican Communion, Pope Paul VI, out of fidelity to his office of safeguarding the Apostolic Tradition, and also with a view to removing a new obstacle placed in the way of Christian unity, reminded Anglicans of the position of the Catholic Church: "She holds that it is not admissible to ordain women to the priesthood, for very fundamental reasons. These reasons include: the example recorded in the Sacred Scriptures of Christ choosing his Apostles only from among men; the constant practice of the Church, which has imitated Christ in choosing only men; and her living teaching authority which has consistently held that the exclusion of women from the priesthood is in accordance with God's plan for his Church.

...As Paul VI later explained: "The real reason is that, in giving the Church her fundamental constitution, her theological anthropology—thereafter always followed by the Church's Tradition—Christ established things in this way."

In the Apostolic Letter *Mulieris Dignitatem*, I myself wrote in this regard: "In calling only men as his Apostles, Christ acted in a completely free and sovereign manner. In doing so, he exercised the same freedom with which, in all his behavior, he emphasized the dignity and the vocation of women, without conforming to the prevailing customs and to the traditions sanctioned by the legislation of the time."

The Holy Father closes with this solemn declaration:

Wherefore, in order that all doubt may be removed regarding a matter of great importance, a matter

> which pertains to the Church's divine constitution itself, in virtue of my ministry of confirming the brethren (cf. Luke 22:32) I *declare* that the Church has no authority whatsoever to confer priestly ordination on women and that this judgment is to be *definitively* held by all the Church's faithful.[23]

THE WELL-KNOWN QUESTION OF THE DEACONESSES

Theologians have already analyzed the well-known matter of deaconesses so often presented by feminists and reformist authors as proof that women used to be admitted to the Sacrament of Holy Orders.

The reformists generally cite the excerpt of Saint Paul's Epistle to the Romans: "I commend to you Phoebe, our sister, who is [also] in the ministry [deaconess] of the church, that is in Cenchreae."[24]

There is no doubt that deaconesses existed in the early Church. However, their role should be made clear. They were matrons who, for the sake of decorum, helped with the baptism of women, which used to be done by immersion, entering the water with them, supporting them and anointing them with oil. They also helped with the catechesis of women, visited young women who were sick, accompanied women when they had to talk to a bishop, presbyters, or deacons, indicated their place in church, made sure they would not fall asleep during ceremonies (in the early times, due to the persecutions, celebrations were held in the wee hours of the night) and so on.

---

23. John Paul II, Apostolic Letter *Ordinatio Sacerdotalis*, www.vatican.va/holy_father/john_paul_ii/apost_letters/documents/hf_jp-ii_apl_22051994_ordinatio-sacerdotalis_en.html. Our emphasis. Cf. Congregation for Doctrine of Faith, *Inter Insigniores*.
24. Rom. 16:1.

Deaconesses were generally widows, consecrated virgins, or spouses of presbyters, bishops, and deacons.[25] The Council of Chalcedon (451) established that women should be at least 40 years old to be consecrated as deaconesses.[26]

There was a rite for the consecration of a deaconess. In it the bishop laid his hands and said a prayer invoking the Holy Spirit. This rite was similar to that used to consecrate deacons. However, Father Solá says, "this consecration was never understood as a true sacrament and women were never considered as part of the clergy."[27] Saint Epiphanius further testifies: "Deaconesses were not instituted in the Church to exert priestly or administrative functions but to tend to, and protect, the modesty of women."[28]

In certain places, the laying of hands by a bishop was erroneously considered as the imposition of Holy Orders. However Herbert Thurston in *The Catholic Encyclopedia* points out that these abuses were repressed without difficulty by the Church through conciliar decrees. Thus, the 19th canon of the Council of Nicaea declared that deaconesses were lay persons and had not received any form of ordination. Mr. Thurston concludes: "It follows from what has been said that the Church as a whole repudiated the idea that women could in any proper sense be recipients of the Sacrament of Order."[29]

---

25. See Chapter 11.
26. For a widow to be admitted to this consecration, Saint Paul recommended that she be at least 60 years old, of good morals, having married only once, and having given a good upbringing to her children (1 Tim. 5:9).
27. Solá, *De sacramentis vitae socialis christianae seu De sacramentis ordinis et matrimonii*, in *Sacrae Theologiae Summa*, p. 646. He also says the consecration of deaconesses was a type of sacramental similar to the blessing received by abbesses (*idem.*, p. 702).
28. Fr. Christian Pesch, S.J., *Parelectiones Dogmaticae* (Friburg: Herder & Co., 1920), p. 303.
29. Herbert Thurston, *s.v.* "Deaconesses," *Catholic Encyclopedia*, Vol. IV, p. 652.

PRESBYTERA, PRESBYTERISSA, AND *EPISCOPA*

The expressions *presbytera*, *presbyterissa*, and *episcopa* appear in some ancient documents. "*Presbytera*" could refer to an elderly woman (*presbytero* meaning elder); a widow (who was usually an older person); a presbyter's wife[30] (who would retire to a community of women and usually become a deaconess); or, at times, it could refer to an abbess. "*Episcopa*" referred to the spouse of a bishop (who would also retire to a community of women) and is well-known in reference to the mother of Pope Saint Paschal I. She was buried with him in Rome's Santa Prassede cemetery.

"Therefore," Father Solá concludes, "*Episcopa*, like *presbytera*, could designate the mother of a bishop or presbyter."[31]

NOT EVEN MARY MOST HOLY RECEIVED THE SACRAMENT OF HOLY ORDERS

Although He loved the Blessed Mother more than anything in Creation, Our Lord did not give Her the priestly character. Nor did He give it to Saint Catherine of Siena, Saint Teresa of Avila, and Saint Thérèse of Lisieux, although they are Doctors of the Church and great among the Saints of Heaven.

We conclude with Father Baker:

> For these and other reasons women cannot and therefore never will be ordained priests (or priestesses) in the Catholic Church. Scripture is against it; tradition is against it. Why? Because it is against God's will and therefore a theological impossibility.[32]

30. See Chapter 11.
31. Solá, *De sacramentis vitae socialis christianae seu De sacramentis ordinis et matrimonii*, in *Sacrae Theologiae Summa*, p. 647.
32. Baker, *Fundamentals of Catholicism*, p. 333.

Conclusion

Many readers will ask what they can specifically do to resolve this crisis assailing the Church in our country.

We would answer that the first step is to understand the crisis properly. This means understanding both its manifestations and implications, while avoiding the media's sensationalist simplifications.

These pages have been written with this in mind. We have analyzed both the theological and practical elements of the crisis, dealing with the issues we believe are at the core of the debate.

We have seen that the backdrop for these scandals is a profound crisis within the Church. From the theological perspective, we have seen why God permits such crises. We have defended the Church's hierarchical nature and demonstrated the utter impossibility of women priests. Among the more practical aspects, we have analyzed the media's role and victim manipulation in the present crisis.

A proper understanding of the crisis unfolds naturally to a state of prayer. Indeed, while practical measures must be taken, it is from God alone that we can expect a true solution and succor in this trial. Without special graces of conversion for both clergy and laity alike, little will be accomplished.[1]

As a second step, then, after understanding the crisis properly, we must pray, and pray ardently. "The kingdom of Heaven suffereth violence, and the violent bear it away."[2] Let us pray with ardor and perseverance for the restoration of the glory and dignity of the Catholic name, for the Hierarchy, the priesthood, and all the faithful.

Finally, we must also fight. In truth, we must pray and fight

1. "And they went forth, and entered into the ship: and that night they caught nothing" John 21:3.
2. Matt. 11:12.

at the same time.

What is the nature of this fight? It is a battle for souls and, thus, fundamentally, a battle to clarify the confusion surrounding the scandals.

Citing the crystal-clear and unchangeable doctrine of the Church, this book has aimed at providing the elements for this effort. Let us put the book to work and use it well.

When reformers come and present their arguments for undermining the Church, we can counter their egalitarian and subversive agenda with the doctrine contained in this work.

When faithful Catholics are impressed by victims and "survivors" aided by the media, we can use the material in this book to expose the tactics of those who would try to capitalize on this sympathy to push for democratic reforms of the Church's hierarchical structure.

When the distinction between the scandalous behavior of individual bishops and the sacredness of their episcopal office is blurred, this book can provide us with arguments for defending the office while we abhor the behavior.

We can speak out with courage and confidence, because by citing the traditional teachings of the Supreme Magisterium of the Church, we cannot err.

We can refute all the false alternatives and call for authentic reform. The reform needed does not entail tearing down the Church's hierarchical form of government, but reforming souls.

Our work is cut out for us. We are not called solely to a crusade of prayer but also to a crusade of clarifying action. The doctrinal and practical considerations in this book are the arms that will aid us in this fray. The battlefield is everywhere around us.

Family members, friends, fellow parishioners, co-workers, and Catholics everywhere need a word of clarity and encouragement. Many already find themselves lying wounded and disheartened by the media barrage that showers upon us. Many more will fall discouraged if they are not forewarned about the enemy's tactics and armed adequately against them.

We cannot let the attacks of those who take the unfortunate path of "reforming" Church doctrine and structures go unopposed. Rather, we must take the offensive and proudly affirm what the Church has always taught. There is no Catholic who cannot help in this crusade of prayer and action.

In this crusade, we must, as Saint Ignatius would say, labor as if victory depended on us alone and not at all on God, attributing victory, when it comes, to God alone and not to our efforts.

Great was the effort made all over Catholic Europe in 1571 to assemble a fleet that could face the threatening Moslems at the high-water mark of their naval power. Despite the Herculean efforts of Pope Saint Pius V, Spain, Venice, Genoa, Naples, and the Knights of Malta, the Catholic fleet that engaged the Turkish vessels in the Gulf of Lepanto on October 7, 1571, was greatly outnumbered. Before the battle, Saint Pius V had asked for public prayers. When victory came, he attributed it entirely to the intercession of Mary, Help of Christians and, in humble gratitude, he instituted the feast of Our Lady of Victory on the first Sunday of October, which Pope Gregory XIII later redesignated as the Feast of the Most Holy Rosary.

We must likewise labor arduously, even if our victory, unlike that at Lepanto, has already been assured. In Fatima, Our Lady identified herself as "the Lady of the Rosary" and promised us her final victory: "Finally, my Immaculate Heart will triumph!"

There is a mysterious relationship between the Blessed Virgin Mary and the Holy Church. Mary is at once the model for the Church and the Mother of the Church. As Prof. Plinio Corrêa de Oliveira wisely noted, because of this mysterious and intimate relationship, there can be no triumph of Mary's

Immaculate Heart without a corresponding triumph of the Church.

It is this mutual triumph that we are all invited to witness, provided we weather the raging storm, proclaiming with our whole heart and soul, amid the heaving waves and howling winds,

Credo in unam, sanctam, catolicam et apostolicam Ecclesiam!

I believe in One, Holy, Catholic, and Apostolic Church!

This TFP paper was published as a full-page ad in *The Wanderer* on April 24, 1997

Appendix A

Is Sodomy No Longer A Sin?

An Urgent Appeal to Our Ecclesiastical Authorities

And the men of Sodom were very wicked, and sinners before the face of the Lord, beyond measure (Gen. 13:13)

I. FALSE SCIENCE, TRUE EVIL

A Standard of Sin

In our dark days, homosexuality, a shameful vice ever abhorred by the Christian conscience, finds prominent apologists within the very bosom of Holy Mother Church.

Sacred Scripture,[1] Tradition, and the Magisterium have condemned few sins more consistently or severely than sodomy. The sins of Sodom and Gomorrha established a measure of evil by which other sins are judged, as recorded throughout the Holy Bible.[2]

Turning a deaf ear to these condemnations, proponents of perversion seek to sow confusion within the Church. To this end, they invoke deceptive interpretations—revisionist distortions—of Sacred Scripture. According to their self-serving rewriting of biblical history, Sodom and Gomorrha were destroyed not because their inhabitants practiced unnatural vice, but because they were inhospitable to travelers.[3]

---

1. Gen. 18:20; 19:12-13, 24-25, 27-28.
2. Lev. 18:22-29; Is. 3:9; Rom. 1:24-27, 32; 1 Cor. 6:9-10; 1 Tim. 1:9-10; 2 Pet. 2:6-9; Jude 1:7.
3. Robert Nugent and Jeannine Gramick, *Building Bridges* (Mystic, Conn.:

Sodomy's apologists have even dared to suggest the obscene blasphemy that Our Lord Jesus Christ was one of them. Sister Jeannine Gramick, co-founder of New Ways Ministry for Gay and Lesbian Catholics, has written:

> Gay and lesbian people also look to the friendships of David and Jonathan, and Jesus and John. These stories hold up for lesbian and gay people a hope for a blessing for same-sex relationships or friendships.[4]

Pseudo-Science

The promoters of the homosexual agenda within the Church profess a pseudo-science in which homosexuality is neither pathological nor reversible, but a genetic and biological trait. According to this parody of science, sexual intimacy with the same sex is simply a normal variation, like left-handedness.

This deceptive fiction has been demolished by a number of systematic studies.[5] It is also contradicted by the fact that a growing number of homosexuals have been treated and freed from the chains of their morally and psychologically disordered compulsions.[6]

Now, the militant call for homosexuals to "come out of the closet" and affirm their vice is being parroted within the ranks of the hierarchy.

In defense of the good name of our beloved Church, of the

Twenty-Third Publications, 1995), p. 10.

4. Sr. Jeannine Gramick, "Can Gays and Lesbians Come Out to Be Faithful Catholics?" *U.S. Catholic*, Aug. 1992, p. 11.
5. See Charles W. Socarides, M.D., *Homosexuality: A Freedom Too Far* (Phoenix: Adam Margrave Books, 1995).
6. For information on how one can turn away from homosexuality, contact one of the following organizations: Beyond Rejection Ministries, Hemet, Calif., 714-925-0028; Courage, New York, N.Y., 212-421-0426; Homosexuals Anonymous Fellowship Services, Redding, Calif., 1-800-253-3000.

moral order ordained by Her Divine Founder, and of the innocent victims of this abominable vice, the American Society for the Defense of Tradition, Family and Property (TFP), appeals to the successors of the Apostles to combat this scandal and the scourge from which it arises.[7]

II. SODOMY: SIGN OF THE CHURCH'S "SELF-DESTRUCTION"

The Popes Speak

The homosexual wreckers within the Church must be viewed in the sad and somber context of Her "self-destruction," of which Pope Paul VI observed:

> The Church finds herself in an hour of disquiet, of self-criticism, one might even say of self-destruction. It is like an acute and complex interior upheaval, which no one expected after the Council. One thought of a blossoming, a serene expansion of the mature concepts of the Council. The Church still has this aspect of blossoming. But since "bonum ex integra causa, malum ex quocumque defectu," the aspect of sorrow has become most notable. The Church is also being wounded by those who are part of her.[8]

7. In so doing we are exercising the right and duty proclaimed in Canon 212, § 3: "In accord with the knowledge, competence and preeminence which they [the Christian faithful] possess, they have the right and even at times a duty to manifest to the sacred pastors their opinion on matters which pertain to the good of the Church, and they have a right to make their opinion known to the other Christian faithful, with due regard for the integrity of faith and morals and reverence towards their pastors, and with consideration for the common good and dignity of persons." James A. Coriden, Thomas J. Green, and Donald E. Heintschel, eds., *The Code of Canon Law, A Text and Commentary* (New York: Paulist Press, 1985).
8. Paul VI, "Allocution to the students of the Lombard Seminary," Dec. 7, 1968, *Insegnamenti di Paolo VI*, vol. 10, pp. 707-709.

His warning finds an empathetic echo in the soul of our Holy Father, who describes this self-destruction in our day:

> One must be realistic and acknowledge with a deep and pained sentiment that a great part of today's Christians feel lost, confused, perplexed, and even disillusioned: ideas contradicting the revealed and unchanging Truth have been spread far and wide; outright heresies in the dogmatic and moral fields have been disseminated, creating doubt, confusion, and rebellion; even the liturgy has been altered. Immersed in intellectual and moral "relativism" and therefore in permissiveness, Christians are tempted by atheism, agnosticism, a vaguely moralistic illuminism, a sociological Christianity, without defined dogmas and without objective morality.[9]

Wolves in Sheep's Clothing

Homosexual predators, calling themselves "Catholic" while violating the most basic norms of Christian morals, further the "self-destruction" of the Church. Their predation is rendered more deadly by the aid and comfort they receive from nuns, priests, and even bishops. Ravening wolves thus devour the weakest of the flock abandoned by their shepherds.

The American TFP commends *The Wanderer* for its service to the faithful in publishing Paul Likoudis's detailed and enlightening reports on the Mass celebrated for unrepentant homosexuals by Rochester's Bishop Matthew Clark in the Cathedral of the Sacred Heart[10] and on the New Ways Ministry 4th National Symposium in Pittsburgh.[11] The sad history

9. John Paul II, "Allocution to the religious and priests participating in the First Italian National Congress on Missions to the People for the 80s," *L'Osservatore Romano*, Feb. 7, 1981.
10. *The Wanderer*, Mar. 1, 1997.
11. Ibid., Mar. 20, 1997.

chronicled by Mr. Likoudis amply evidences the homosexual revolution that threatens our Church and our Nation.

III. THE SODOMITES' STRATEGY: AVOID CAUSING A REACTION

New Ways for Old Sins

The New Ways Ministry conference set the homosexual lobby's plan of action, emphasizing the strategy of gradualism that marks the homosexual revolution. The objective of the sodomites' strategy is to avoid meaningful reaction by ecclesiastical authorities against the homosexual agenda.

Bishop Clark, in his tweed-suit and striped-shirt "clericals," encouraged conference participants: "If individuals change quite slowly, how slow is institutional change?" Driving home his brother bishop's message to those he dubbed "a loving group," Detroit Auxiliary Bishop Thomas Gumbleton added, "As Matthew said, even if we are frustrated sometimes with the slowness of change, we still must put up with that frustration as we continue to struggle to make it happen."[12]

Step-by-Step: The Descent Into Hell

In the moral realm, the homosexual revolution proclaims the view that the sexual ethics professed by the Church are inevitably evolving to the stage where homosexual relations will be equal—if not superior—to heterosexual intimacy.

Prof. Joseph Selling, chairman of the Department of Moral Theology at the Catholic University of Louvain, gave the symposium a progress report on the gradualist strategy for the Church's acceptance of sodomy.

12. Bishop Matthew Clark and Bishop Thomas Gumbleton, "Pastoral Care of Lesbian and Gay People," Plenary Session, New Ways Ministry 4th National Symposium, Pittsburgh, March 7-9, 1997.

> Is the teaching going to continue to evolve? With respect to the homosexual relationship, will it evolve toward encompassing it? Yes, it will! We have already taken the first step. Begrudgingly as we might like to admit, even the teaching of the Church has recognized the homosexual person, the homosexual orientation. It may be very uncomfortable with its own statements, but it's there! The homosexual person is a person and no less of a person than anyone else. This is the first step. The second step is the recognition of the homosexual relationship. I think we are virtually on the edge of accepting the homosexual relationship. The Church will accept the homosexual relationship, like those divorced and remarried: We must live as brother and sister or brother and brother and sister and sister as the case may be... [The audience laughs.] What is important is that the relationship be recognized as a valuable, fruitful, meaningful, affirmative, creative relationship. We are on the verge of accepting this. The third step is: Can we accept the homosexual act? Before we can talk about the morality of the homosexual act, we have to define it, to understand exactly what it is.... Our whole understanding of human sexuality needs to be rewritten, but rewritten not from a "procreative or reproductive" point of view. It needs to be rewritten from a "relational" point of view.[13]

Gradualism was a thread woven throughout the fabric of the New Ways for old sins symposium, as was the abhorrence sterile vice accords fruitful love. Sr. Margaret Farley, R.S.M., of Yale University, made clear the reason for the sodomites' fear

13. Joseph Selling, "The Meanings of Human Sexuality," New Ways Ministry 4th National Symposium.

and loathing of the sacramental love that gives birth to life and preserves chastity.

> As long as the Christian sexual ethic was focused on "procreation" and the "control of sexual desire," there was no room for a positive evaluation of homosexuality. But in recent decades, under the pressure of new discoveries in the social sciences and scientific fields, traditional Catholic sexual morality is crumbling. Now, the "procreative norm" is gone, the rigid stereotype of male/female complementarity is gone, and the time is ripe for a positive evaluation of homosexuality and same-sex relations.[14]

A Homosexual Pastoral

Religion provides the surest yardstick by which human acts may be measured. Unlike such continua as healthy/diseased, virtuous/sinful reflects a transcendent reality that bears directly on conscience. Sinfulness is a particularly relevant construct since it addresses not only an act's rationality but also its effects on the universal order.

The moral standards taught by religion are the single most important factor in the virtually universal rejection of homosexual vice. Accordingly, those promoting the homosexual agenda strive to change the traditional Church teachings that constitute its principal obstacle.

Astute sodomites know that before changes can deconstruct and deviate doctrine, they must be put into practice. According to the homosexual revolution, pastoral practice should not be governed by Christian sexual ethics but by an erroneous view of social justice in which the Church has the duty to defend the

14. Sr. Margaret Farley, R.S.M., "Same-Sex Relations: An Ethical Perspective," New Ways Ministry 4th National Symposium.

civil rights of practicing homosexuals as homosexuals.[15]

Fr. Richard Peddicord, O.P., professor of moral theology at the Aquinas Institute of Theology in St. Louis, described the rationale for a homosexual pastoral at the New Ways symposium.

> Catholic sexual ethics do not have the conceptual tools to say how homosexuals should be treated by civil society. The issue of homosexual rights should be considered under social justice.[16]

A homosexual pastoral, Father Peddicord continued, "should not be satisfied with repeating the moral condemnations of gay sex, but advance the civil rights of homosexuals."

According to its advocates, a homosexual pastoral "should provide a supportive atmosphere for a stable relationship." A significant step in this direction was taken by certain "pastoral guidelines" that defend "the stable, faithful, and committed homosexual relationships" as "a better moral situation than promiscuity."[17]

As early as 1979, the bishops of England and Wales offered

---

15. The Congregation for the Doctrine of the Faith states in "Some Considerations Concerning the Response to Legislative Proposals on the Non-discrimination of Homosexual Persons," of July 22, 1992: "Including `homosexual orientation' among the considerations on the basis of which it is illegal to discriminate can easily lead to regarding homosexuality as a positive source of human rights, for example, in respect to so-called affirmative action or preferential treatment in hiring practices. This is all the more deleterious since there is no right to homosexuality, which therefore should not form the basis for judicial claims. The passage from the recognition of homosexuality as a factor on which basis it is illegal to discriminate can easily, if not automatically, lead to the legislative protection and promotion of homosexuality. A person's homosexuality would be invoked in opposition to alleged discrimination, and thus the exercise of rights would be defended precisely via the affirmation of the homosexual condition instead of in terms of a violation of basic human rights" (no. 13).
16. Fr. Richard Peddicord, O.P., "Catholic Moral Teaching on Gay and Lesbian Rights Legislation," New Ways Ministry 4th National Symposium.
17. Nugent and Gramick, *Building Bridges*, p. 143.

pastoral guidelines urging pastors to distinguish between "irresponsible, indiscriminate sexual activity and the permanent association between two homosexual persons who feel incapable of enduring a solitary life devoid of sexual expression."[18]

In the homosexual pastoral, the distinction between "homosexual orientation" and "homosexual behavior" is challenged. "The bishops," according to Fr. Robert Nugent and Sr. Jeannine Gramick, honestly acknowledge that the difference is "not always clearly convincing." They are undoubtedly aware that while many people find the distinction useful in teaching and counseling programs on homosexuality, they do not find it particularly helpful in the pastoral field or fully congruent with the experiences of gay and lesbian Catholics.[19]

A New Liberation Theology

In 1969, the Stonewall Riots in New York City unleashed a major homosexual offensive. From this disorder sprang "lesbian/gay theology," which now dominates many Catholic universities and seminaries.

Like liberation theology, much in vogue in Latin America before the collapse of the Soviet Union, homosexual theology is a "theology from below." Both theologies arise from a praxis (experience) and a purportedly scientific analysis of that experience.

Liberation theology used Marxist analysis of the socioeconomic conditions in Third World countries to establish its theological and hermeneutical principles, which provided a sympathetic ideology for guerrilla movements fighting to impose communism on their fellow man.

Homosexual theology is a new liberation theology that uses the praxis of the "lesbian/gay experience" to liberate man from

18. Catholic Social Welfare Commission (Britain), 1981, p. 8.
19. Nugent and Gramick, *Building Bridges*, p. 144.

the bonds of Christian morals.

As Father Nugent and Sister Gramick, the co-founders of New Ways Ministry, boast, lesbian/gay theology is an example of authentic subversion. It involves a real turning from below with a scriptural analysis from the underside of society. Since God's spirit is continually revealing truth to the human heart, the scriptures contain some insights that can be made known to the Christian community only through the testimony of lesbian and gay people.[20]

Such a spurious interpretation of Sacred Scripture was echoed by Bishop Gumbleton at the New Ways symposium.

> I learned from reading an article by Andrew Sullivan in *America* magazine a few years ago, where he was speaking about his own experience of learning how to love within his context of being a gay man. When he was asked by his friend, "Do you really believe that what we are doing is wrong? Because if you do, I cannot go on with this," he says, "Of course I was forced to say I do not believe at some level." You see what Andrew Sullivan is telling us? He found God in his experience as a gay man. We know that God is love, and where there is love, there is God. And Andrew Sullivan tells us that his experience is that he finds God where he finds love.[21]

Call to Action: "Come Out!"

Declaring that "The time is ripe," Bishop Gumbleton called on homosexuals "to share their gifts" with fellow Catholics since "this is how our Church is going to change."

---

20. Ibid., p. 190.
21. Bishops Clark and Gumbleton, "Pastoral Care of Lesbians and Gay People."

The most important thing that we can do in our pastoral care is to create a church community where gay, lesbian, bisexual, and transgendered people can be truly open about who they are.... I think it is very, very important that they experience a warmth and oneness within the Church to allow them to share their gifts with our Church.... I encourage this because I hope that within our Church, every gay person, every lesbian person, every bisexual or transgendered person will come out, because that is how our Church is going to truly change: when everyone who from this community of homosexual people is courageous enough, because it does take courage to come out.... I would say this especially to bishops and priests within our Church. I cannot tell you the number of letters I have received in the last few years from priests who say they are gay, but are afraid to come out. What a loss this is to our Church! Because if they were willing to stand up on a Sunday morning in front of their community and to say who they really are, our Church could much more fully and quickly appreciate the gifts that homosexuals can bring to the whole community of our Church and to our society as well.... As more and more people come out, more families are changed, more churches are changed, more parishes are changed, and our whole Church is changed. And so I appeal here publicly to all of us within the Church to create a community in which this can happen. But then, for those who are gay or lesbian or bisexual or transgendered, please come forward. Say who you are, be proud of who you are, and share all of your gifts with our Church.[22]

22. Ibid.

IV. Invoking the Abyss

As an uncompromised champion of the Faith, Prof. Plinio Corrêa de Oliveira advises in his seminal treatise *Revolution and Counter-Revolution:*

> Disordered passions, moving in a crescendo analogous to the acceleration of gravity and feeding upon their own works, lead to consequences which in their turn develop according to a proportional intensity. In like progression, errors beget errors, and revolutions prepare the way for revolutions.... This explains why we find ourselves today in such a paroxysm of impiety and immorality and such an abyss of disorder and discord.[23]

Sacred Scripture warns, "*Abyssus abyssum invocat*"—"Deep calleth on deep" (Ps. 41:8).

"Celebrate Diversity" proclaims a bumper sticker popular among the sodomites and their apologists. The practice of homosexual vice inevitably descends into the lowest depths of the moral abyss. From pedophilia to sadomasochism, any and all abominations—even bestiality—find justification in the perverse school of sexual deviance. In the upside-down world of the homosexual pastoral, could a homosexual "find God" through the "interspecies love" of bestiality? Such questions are only prudent in view of the fact that we are witnessing the gradual acceptance of homosexuality as a legitimate way of life, not only in secular society but within the Church. This process of self-destruction—of Church and State—constitutes an authentic and cataclysmic revolution to which we are unalterably opposed.

23. *Revolution and Counter-Revolution*, 3rd ed. (York, Penn.: The American TFP, 1993), p. 30.

V. AN APPEAL TO OUR ECCLESIASTICAL AUTHORITIES

Along with contraception, abortion, and euthanasia, homosexual vice is an integral weapon of the Culture of Death aimed at our families, our Nation, and our Church.

In face of this danger to all we hold dear, the American Society for the Defense of Tradition, Family, and Property, comprised of practicing Catholics dedicated to defending the moral standards of Christian civilization, is obliged to publicly appeal to our ecclesiastical authorities to employ urgent and energetic measures against the advance of the homosexual agenda within the Church.

We also respectfully direct our appeal to the Congregation for the Doctrine of the Faith, filially imploring this sacred dicastery to effectively denounce and condemn the pernicious doctrinal errors against Catholic morality that are being taught with impunity in many dioceses and seminaries, as well as in Catholic schools and universities across the country.

In so doing, we defend our beloved Nation against the perversion and loss of its soul. We also defend our even more beloved Holy Mother Church by demanding that Her clergy, and in particular Her bishops, teach what the Church and Her Divine Master teach.

May the Blessed Virgin Mary, conceived without sin, Patroness of the United States, protect us from this terrible onslaught of perversity.

The American Society for the Defense of
Tradition, Family and Property—(TFP)

This TFP paper was first published as a full-page ad in *The Washington Times*, April 11, 2002

Appendix B

In Face of the Scandals, The Church, Holy and Immortal, Shall Prevail!

"Thou art Peter; and upon this rock I will build My Church, and the gates of Hell shall not prevail against Her" (Matt. 16:18). To this first promise, Our Lord added a second: "Heaven and earth will pass away, but My words will not pass away" (Matt. 24:35). Thus did Jesus Christ establish the One Holy Roman Catholic and Apostolic Church, sealing Her immortality with His divine guarantee.

The violence of the storm currently assailing the Church would likely bring down many a human institution, but not the institution supported by God's own promises. The Church's enemies try with all their might to defame and dishonor Her. They hurl mud and muck, but they fail to sully Her.

They declare that She cannot survive the scandals perpetrated within and against Her, but their words ring with the uncertainty that it will indeed be so. Confronted with the silent testimony of history, they know by experience that the Church is both holy and immortal. Nothing stains Her, not even infamy rising from Her ranks, for She is the spotless Bride of Christ.

Even at the height of His passion—when the insults against His Divine Person, the wounds inflicted on His Sacred Body, and His public humiliation had reached their apex—the Word of God Incarnate lost none of the grandeur in His moral profile. We see this in the Holy Shroud of Turin. Here is a Man atrociously wounded, one would almost say crushed, yet, no painting or sculpture of a king presents more majesty, dignity, or honor than the figure stamped on that burial cloth.

BETRAYED IGNOBLY FROM WITHIN, ATTACKED FIERCELY FROM WITHOUT

So it is with the Catholic Church today. At the height of Her passion, betrayed ignobly from within, attacked fiercely from without, nothing can disturb Her serenity. When this frightful storm finally abates, She will appear again radiant and victorious.

But while the storm lasts, the suffering is intense, and our faith is tested. For us Catholics this means the shocking realization that a hostile element, a horrendous cancer, grows within the Mystical Body of Christ. We shudder at the tragic and unnatural "peaceful coexistence" between vice and that which is virtuous and holy.

The existence of homosexuality[1] in the institution that is the very soul of purity and chastity is deplorable beyond words. Equally deplorable is the fact that this "peaceful coexistence" has lasted for decades due to the unpardonable connivance of shepherds who should have been ready to lay down their lives if necessary to prevent this evil from gaining access to the fold.

The *Catechism of St. Pius X* calls homosexuality a sin that "cries out to Heaven for vengeance,"[2] and the *Catechism of the Catholic Church* promulgated by Pope John Paul II in 1992 says: "Basing itself on Sacred Scripture, which presents homosexual acts as acts of grave depravity, tradition has always declared that 'homosexual acts are intrinsically disordered.'"[3] Homosexuality is a sin condemned in the Old Testament[4] and

1. In opposition to a usage that is becoming generalized, we restrict the term "homosexuality" to homosexual practices, thus excluding the mere inclination. No individual who suffers from such unnatural inclination and resists it with the help of grace can be called a "homosexual," just as no one who resists the inclination to steal or lie can be called a "thief," or a "liar."
2. Cf. www.ewtn.com/library/catechism/PiusXCat.txt. Theologians give Gen. 19:13 as the scriptural basis for this designation.
3. *Catechism of the Catholic Church* (New York: Doubleday, 1995) ¶ 2357, p. 625.
4. Cf. Gen. 19:1-29; Lev. 18:22; Deut. 22:5.

by both Saint Peter and Saint Paul in the New,[5] by Fathers and Doctors of the Church, and by the Popes for 2,000 years. Saint Peter Damian, Doctor of the Church, says it "should not be considered an ordinary vice, for it surpasses all of them in enormity."[6]

We speak of homosexuality, for this indeed is the problem. We all know the truth: The vast majority of the exposed scandals are cases of pedophiliac homosexuality, and thus a particularly heinous spillover of the more widespread problem of homosexuality. Large sectors of the media, however, choose to gloss over the homosexuality and highlight the pedophilia.[7]

This same media have no qualms about unleashing a ferocious uproar against the Church, Her doctrine and morals. Adding insult to injury, they give the impression that the criminal behavior of some is the general rule. This is a supreme injustice to all the priests and religious who are faithful to their vows. Moreover, they suggest that the scandals exist because of clerical celibacy. Callously oblivious to the faith and feeling of one billion Catholics, they make scant attempt to show the other side of the coin, namely the sublimity of the Catholic priesthood as reflected in its saints down through the ages.

A MYSTERIOUS PROCESS OF "SELF-DESTRUCTION"

Let us put aside, however, this external assault on the Church and focus on the more important problem within.

The first step in solving any problem consists in its thorough

5. Cf. 2 Pet. 2:6-7; Rom. 1:24-27; 1 Cor. 6:10; 1 Tim. 1:10.
6. St. Peter Damian, *The Book of Gomorrah* (*Patrologia Latina*, Vol. 145, col. 159-190) quoted in Roberto de Mattei, *L'Église et l'homosexualité* (Paris: Pierre Téqui Éditeur, 1995), p. 12.
7. Pedophilia is frequently, albeit not necessarily, connected with homosexuality. This is certainly the case with the current scandals, wherein almost all of the prepubescent children molested by clergy were boys. The homosexual abuse of teen-age boys is pederasty (ephebophilia).

and accurate analysis. Then we can see its detrimental consequences and especially its root cause.

The problem would not exist but for the most culpable negligence of numerous shepherds and, in some cases, the most condemnable complicity of others. There is much for the clergy to address within its ranks, vigorously and urgently. Oh, how many tears will turn to joy when the faithful see bishops like our glorious Saint John Neumann, Philadelphia's fourth (1852-1860), fearlessly taking on those who would harm Christ's "little flock." It behooves us all to beseech God earnestly to send saints and heroes to teach, govern, and sanctify His flock.

Is the clergy alone responsible, though? Is there not the possibility that we—the Catholic laity—stand to be blamed as well, if in varying degrees? Surely, we trusted in the watchfulness of our shepherds. Surely, we feel that our trust was betrayed. Nevertheless, Our Lord had more than just the shepherds in mind when He said, "Watch and pray, that you enter not into temptation" (Matt. 26:41); He addressed us as well.

Did we "watch and pray?" Unfortunately not. In the Garden of Olives, we would have been among those who slept. If our analysis is to be honest we must acknowledge this.

Decades ago, Pope Paul VI warned that "the smoke of Satan" had entered the Church.[8] He also said that She was undergoing a mysterious process of "self-destruction."[9] Did we take this warning to heart? Did we investigate this mysterious process? Its methods? How it affected both clergy and faithful?

We let this "smoke of Satan" fill every nook and cranny in the Church. Like a stupefying gas it relaxed and anesthetized us. It diminished our fighting spirit. Indifference became gen-

8. Cf. Allocution *Resistite fortes in fide*, of June 29, 1972, in *Insegnamenti di Paolo VI* (Vatican: Poliglotta Vaticana), Vol. 10, pp. 707-709.
9. Cf. Allocution to the students of the Pontifical Lombard Seminary on December 7, 1968, in *Insegnamenti di Paolo VI*, Vol. 6, p. 1188.

eralized, and the process of "self-destruction" was left free to do its nefarious work. Today we see the consequences.

This "smoke of Satan" also spread intellectual and moral "relativism" throughout the Church.[10] This relativism spared nothing: the sublime vocation and sacred persons of priest and bishop; the respectful and prayerful atmosphere within churches; the rules of beauty in Church art and architecture; the reverence due to consecrated religious life; the rules of modesty in dress, not only in public but even in our churches; and so much more. All that elevated the souls of the faithful, all that filled them with admiration and veneration for the supernatural, was targeted.

Inevitably this relativism slowly weakened in consciences the notions of good and evil, sin and grace, vice and virtue. The Church's clear teaching on every aspect of sexual behavior was gradually blurred. Virtue was replaced with a pathetic feel-good spirituality, so that eventually we fell to where we are today, proof positive of the existence of a process dubbed "satanic" by a Pope in our own lifetime.

Some critics, moved more by emotions and force of habit than clear thinking, will deny this process of "self-destruction." Unfortunately, the media bring us daily a most palpable sign of its continuation: Seeing the Church so hard pressed by the scandals, Her enemies both within and without are quick to clamor for additional "reform." In open challenge to Her Supreme Magisterium, they demand that the Church abolish clerical celibacy and accept the ordination of women, divorce, contraception, abortion, and, oddly enough, even homosexual-

10. Moral "relativism" tries to adapt Catholic doctrine and morality to one's personal fancies or the ruling form of worldliness. Objective norms of thought and action are thus destroyed. The person becomes the slave of his own caprices and those of fashion, as channeled by the media. Eventually, he accepts evil in the guise of good. Cf. Pope John Paul II's Allocution to the religious and priests participating in the First Italian National Congress on Missions to the People for the '80s, *L'Osservatore Romano*, Feb. 7, 1981.

ity. This is exactly what the Church should not do! This would be the next step toward the abyss of total relativism.

RETRACING OUR STEPS

There is only one way to extricate ourselves from the problem we are in—now that our eyes are open. We must retrace our steps. We must return from whence we came. Only in the fullness of Church teaching will we find the solution to the present crisis. The Church has dealt with many problems during 2,000 years. She is no less able to deal with them today.

The first and obvious step then is to ***pray***.

The second is to ***watch***, as Our Lord commanded. We must hone our ability to watch, to pay attention to lurking danger. Thus, when danger appears—particularly when in sheep's clothing—we must know how to resist it; we must know how to assess things in the light of Catholic principles. This presupposes a clear understanding of the perennial truths of the Faith and the unchanging principles of morality, for which we must ***study***. This "back to the basics" study of Church teaching will rekindle in our hearts a burning love for all the principles long eroded by relativism.

A CALL FOR HEROISM

The third step is a proper understanding of sanctity—***the heroic struggle for virtue***. True and heroic virtue is not anemic or self-centered. It is full of fruits in the apostolate with others. It rejects the comfort zone and the dictates of human respect—the fear of creating complications for ourselves. When faced with opposition, be it from within or without, it does not cringe and boldly proclaims the Faith and sound doctrine. The truth is not something to be ashamed of. Our Lord wants us to influence society, as yeast ferments the dough. He expects us to be courageous in the face of public ridicule, like Veronica. He invites us to ***heroism***: "Everyone therefore that shall confess Me before men, I will also confess him before My Father Who is in Heaven" (Matt. 10:32).

For this journey back to the paternal home to be successful it must become a true spiritual crusade, with all the dedication, self-sacrifice, and zeal shown by the heroes of old. These answered Blessed Urban II's call to arms at Clermont-Ferrand, when he launched the First Crusade, with reverberating cries of "God wills it! God wills it!"

If this crusading spirit burns within our breasts, our ecclesiastical leaders will have no doubt that they can rely on our enthusiastic support, provided they courageously assail this largely unchallenged process of "self-destruction" with the indispensable vigor of shepherds defending their flock from ravenous wolves.

BEYOND ALL DOUBT, THE CHURCH SHALL PREVAIL

If both clergy and faithful carry out their respective duties, with the unfailing help of the Blessed Virgin Mary, of Saint Joseph, Her most chaste spouse and Protector of the Universal Church, of all the angels and saints, we will be rewarded by seeing the Church win one more battle. The present crisis is but one more episode—even if one of the worst—in Her glorious history of struggles.

We are reminded of this by the Catholic intellectual Prof. Plinio Corrêa de Oliveira, who wrote in his seminal work, *Revolution and Counter-Revolution*: "Amid the storms through which She passes today, the Church could proudly and tranquilly say: 'I have seen other winds, I have beheld other storms.'[11] The Church has fought in other lands, against adver-

11. "Alios ego vidi ventos; alias prospexi animo procellas," Cicero, *Familiares*, 12, 25, 5.

saries from among other peoples, and She will undoubtedly continue to face problems and enemies quite different from those of today until the end of time."[12]

12. *Revolution and Counter-Revolution* (York, Penn.: The American TFP, 1993), p. 115.

This TFP statement was published as an ad in *The Dallas Morning News* on June 13, 2002

Appendix C

Pressure Groups Push for Revolution Inside the Catholic Church

The American Society for the Defense of Tradition, Family and Property—TFP sent the letter below to the nation's bishops to express its concern about reformist pressure groups taking advantage of the present crisis to foment revolution inside the Church.

June 1, 2002

Your Excellency:

Mr. Thomas McKenna, the American TFP's Vice President, recently sent you and all the other bishops a copy of a full-page ad we published in *The Washington Times* on April 11 titled "The Church, Holy and Immortal, Shall Prevail!" This was the first phase of a nationwide campaign to defend the Church in face of the current upheaval. The many bishops who responded were all supportive. In the campaign's second phase, the statement was sent to all 48,000 priests in the country and to 9,000 religious. Currently, our campaign is in its third phase. The statement continues to be published in other papers and distributed in flier form. About 400,000 copies of the enclosed flier have gone out.

In following the news from around the country, we have become painfully concerned as to how the crisis surrounding the sexual-abuse scandals is unfolding. We would like to share these concerns with you and all members of the U.S. hierarchy.

Although the crisis lies more immediately within the spiritual sphere, it also affects profoundly the whole temporal sphere within which the TFP acts.

We are worried, seeing how a reformist pressure movement is beginning to take shape within the ranks of the laity. This movement is taking advantage of the crisis to foment revolution inside the Church, and it enjoys extensive coverage from the secular media.

This subversive intervention is all the more improper if we consider that the real solution has already been given by appropriate authority in the April 23-24 meeting of the American Cardinals with the Pope in Rome. The "Final Statement" issued at the conclusion of this meeting presents clearly both the problem and the effective measures that must be implemented to resolve it. Point 5 of the part on Principles, for example, states:

"**5)** Given the doctrinal issues underlying the deplorable behavior in question, certain lines of response have been proposed:

"**a)** The Pastors of the Church need clearly to promote the correct moral teaching of the Church and publicly to reprimand individuals who spread dissent and groups which advance ambiguous approaches to pastoral care;

"**b)** A new and serious Apostolic Visitation of seminaries and other institutes of formation must be made without delay, with particular emphasis on the need for fidelity to the Church's teaching, especially in the area of morality, and the need for a deeper study of the criteria of suitability of candidates to the priesthood." (*Zenit*, 4/25/02)

We see the crisis being presented quite differently, however, by an alliance of the secular media and reformist pressure groups. From child abuse, the problem becomes Church government and doctrine.

This metastasizing of the problem is illustrated by an affirmation reportedly made by Dr. James Muller: "Pedophilia is only a symptom of a disease. The disease is absolute power" (as quoted by Mary Rourke in *The Los Angeles Times*, 4/23/02). Dr. Muller is the president of Voice of the Faithful, a movement that somehow resembles a poisonous mushroom, for it appeared overnight; it is growing fast thanks to the media and assistance from such long-standing groups as Call to Action; and it holds positions that clash with Church teaching.

To advance its agenda, the media-reformist alliance must first shake the trust of the faithful in their priests and bishops. To achieve this a veritable army of muckrakers was set in motion whose claims and findings are constantly paraded in the public eye. Additional pressure is being brought to bear by orchestrated efforts to seriously undermine Church funding—apparently a Call to Action idea (see Rourke)—thus crippling financial resources already burdened by a growing number of lawsuits seeking damages for sexual abuse. In a vain attempt to legitimize their subversive actions, reformists cast themselves as American patriots, with allusions to "the Boston Tea Party" and the use of slogans like "no donation without representation."

It is from within, and conditioned by this hurricane of pressure, that reformists make their demands: empower the laity; eliminate, curtail, or render meaningless all priestly, episcopal, and Papal authority; make priestly celibacy optional; ordain women; change Church teaching on birth control, divorce, abortion, and homosexuality; and so forth.

In a May 27, 2002, article in *America*, retired Archbishop John R. Quinn of San Francisco compared the present crisis to the Reformation and the French Revolution. Indeed there are analogies, both between those two historical upheavals (cf.

Plinio Corrêa de Oliveira, *Revolution and Counter-Revolution*, 1993, p. 17), and between them and the reformists' agenda today.

For example, reformist pressure groups would love to see the bishops use the Dallas meeting to abdicate from their rights and responsibilities following the example of the French nobility during the French Revolution, on August 4, 1789.

Reformists entertain hopes that Dallas will lead to the creation of lay boards at the national, diocesan, and parish level to "oversee" the clergy. Reformist pressure groups such as Voice of the Faithful advocate "a general assembly of lay people to be consulted, potentially, on **everything** including finances, personnel and liturgy"(Pam Bullock, *The New York Times*, 5/31/02; our emphasis). This "general assembly of lay people" would mirror the Estates General that initiated the revolutionary process that toppled the French monarchy.

Reformists want to create a type of national lay advisory board on sexual abuse, which might parallel the "Committee of Public Safety," the group of revolutionaries that radicalized the process, leading in a short time to the Terror.

Today's reformists look at the clergy the same way the Jacobins looked at the aristocrats during the French Revolution, in other words, as imbecilic, arrogant, oppressive, and corrupt (e.g., Fr. Andrew Greeley, *America*, 5/27/02).

The analogies continue. Reformists see today's laity as the Jacobins saw the *sans culottes* (the revolutionary plebeians): they alone are capable of leading, they alone are virtuous and immaculate. Ironically, the bloodstained plebeian Robespierre was known as "the Incorruptible." Of such stuff, revolutionary myths are made.

Based on our broad contact with American Catholic public opinion, we conclude that these reformist pressure groups do not represent average American Catholics. The latter are often silent, but they love the Church, as holy and immortal today as ever. They love everything associated with the Church. They love the Papacy and the Church's hierarchical structure.

Obviously, this silent majority of American Catholics is deeply hurt by the present crisis. Their hearts bleed profusely for the victims of so much criminal abuse. Theirs, however, are not the hearts of revolutionary firebrands, but the hearts of sons, the hearts of daughters. American Catholics are hurt, but they are not rebellious.

In and beyond Dallas, the struggle continues between the Church and the media-reformist pressure groups alliance. The American TFP is doing what it can to bring hope and perspective to Catholics across the land. We are moved to do this out of love for the Church, whose hierarchical structure was divinely instituted by Our Lord.

Dallas, however, is the immediate concern. As Your Excellency meets with other bishops to address the crisis, the American TFP's directors, members, friends, and supporters around the country will be praying for you, asking the Holy Spirit, through the intercession of Mary Most Holy, to assist you with His gifts, granting you wisdom and strength to resist heroically the subversive agenda being pushed by the media-reformist alliance.

Asking for your blessing and prayers for our efforts, I remain,

In Jesus and Mary,

Raymond Earl Drake

Raymond Earl Drake
President

Index

The American Society for the Defense of Tradition, Family and Property (TFP) was born of a group of Catholic Americans concerned about the multiple crises shaking every aspect of American life. Founded in 1973, the American TFP was formed to resist, in the realm of ideas, the liberal, socialist and communist trends of the times and proudly affirm the positive values of tradition, family and property. Central to the TFP mission is the idea that the various crises threatening American society and the Catholic Church cannot be seen as separate and disjointed events but rather must be seen as the consequences of a worldwide crisis based on the errors of our times. The TFP handbook *Revolution and Counter-Revolution* by Plinio Corrêa de Oliveira masterfully traces the historical and philosophical roots of the present crisis and proposes a response.

Thus, the TFP is a movement that embraces every field of action, especially in art, ideas and culture. TFP books, publications and newspaper advertisements help bring these views to the public. Moreover, the TFP takes issues to the streets with colorful sidewalk campaigns in major cities.

The first TFP was founded in Brazil in 1960 by Prof. Plinio Corrêa de Oliveira. The American TFP is one of many autonomous TFPs that now exist around the world dedicated to the same ideals and at the service of Christian Civilization. The American TFP's national headquarters is located in Spring Grove, Pennsylvania.

The TFP Committee on American Issues is a study commission recently set up to monitor events in American society and the Church. It issues papers and articles that frequently appear on the TFP website. For more information on the TFP please visit its website at **www.tfp.org**.

Nobility and Analogous Traditional Elites in the Allocutions of Pius XII:

A Theme Illuminating American Social History

by *Plinio Corrêa de Oliveira*

Since the eighteenth century, generations have been schooled in utopian principles proclaiming total equality as the guarantor of liberty and justice for all. The egalitarian myth of a classless society was proffered as the unquestionable path down which mankind must travel to reach perfect social harmony. This book does much to shatter these myths and provide a Catholic approach to the way society should be structured as seen by the Popes.

592 pages, hardcover, 64 full-color pictures, 52 black-and-white pictures, Hamilton Press, ©1993. **$49.95**

Revolution and Counter-Revolution

by *Plinio Corrêa de Oliveira*

If anything characterizes our times, it is a sense of pervading chaos. In every field of human endeavor, the windstorms of change are fast altering the ways we live. Contemporary man is no longer anchored in certainties and thus has lost sight of who he is, where he comes from and where he is going. If there is a single book that can shed light amid the postmodern darkness, this is it.

180 pages, softcover, American Society for the Defense of Tradition, Family, and Property (TFP), ©1993. **$9.95**

To order please call: 1-888-317-5571

The Crusader of the 20th Century

by Roberto de Mattei

"With the integrity of his life as an authentic Catholic, Plinio Corrêa de Oliveira offers us a confirmation of the Church's continuing fecundity. The difficulties of these times for true Catholics are, in fact, occasions to influence history by affirming perennial Christian principles. Such was the case with Professor Plinio, the eminent Brazilian thinker who demonstrated it by boldly maintaining, in an age of totalitarianism of every stripe and color, his unshakable faith in the fundamental teachings and institutions of the Church." From the Introduction by Alfonso Cardinal Stickler.

First Edition, 278 pages, hardcover, ©1998. **$14.95**

To order please call: 1-888-317-5571